The Health of Nations

The Health of Nations

✦

Why the Safety of Humanity and Peace in the World Depends on Us All

I. Khan

iUniverse, Inc.
New York Lincoln Shanghai

The Health of Nations
Why the Safety of Humanity and Peace in the World Depends on Us All

iUniverse books may be ordered through booksellers or by contacting:

iUniverse
2021 Pine Lake Road, Suite 100
Lincoln, NE 68512
www.iuniverse.com
1-800-Authors (1-800-288-4677)

Second Edition
Spring 2005

ISBN-13: 978-0-595-31997-8 (pbk)
ISBN-13: 978-0-595-66459-7 (cloth)
ISBN-13: 978-0-595-76803-5 (ebk)
ISBN-10: 0-595-31997-1 (pbk)
ISBN-10: 0-595-66459-8 (cloth)
ISBN-10: 0-595-76803-2 (ebk)

Printed in the United States of America

To my children Sher, Schehrezade, Shaun, and the children of humanity.

Contents

Part III   PROCLAMATION *Messages to the 21st Century from the perspective of Nature's God*

Part IV   EVOLUTION *through a sense of urgency using intellect and diplomacy.*

Part V   EMANCIPATION *from politics as usual.*

Foreword

Iskandar ("I") Khan wanted this book to communicate an urgent and important message that we must shift our way of thinking quickly, get involved and follow a path that would avoid what seemed to him to be almost inevitable. Originally, he became concerned about another major tragic war in the world in 1994 and wrote his thoughts but did not publish them. He thought the human race should take great care, because international stress was likely to result in World War III of the nuclear kind. This book was in its final stages of editing when the author suddenly passed away on January 7, 2004.

Iskandar was originally named Taimur Khan at birth. His father later changed his name at the behest of an astrologer, because he was told that if Taimur grew up with that name, he would be above the intellect of most people, and that he would not be understood. In some respects, it happened anyway. He turned adult without childhood because of the expectations of him. He was always at the top of his class and received many awards of academic excellence in science and engineering. Iskandar was a student, a teacher, a thinker, a philosopher, a scientist, a visionary, an achiever, a businessman, an author, an engineer, a patriarch of a family and a friend to many. Most of all, he was a kind and decent man who considered *The Health of Nations* the beginning of his contribution to the safety of humanity.

The book describes his creation of an Internet-based organization called My Use International (Chapter 16) that is physically based in California. The vision of the organization is a political party of mankind, crossing all geographical and cultural boundaries. He provided this as a forum for worldwide communication and cooperation that would unite individuals of all nationalities under the umbrella of world peace. It would provide thought-provoking entertainment and education through film, publications, DVD and other media to promote mutual understanding among the world's diverse cultures, which is thought to be absolutely essential in achieving a commonality as a prerequisite for peace. The mission is to prevent a nuclear World War III, and to be a significant influence to continuing peace in the world. We, at My Use International, have dedicated ourselves to getting this book published and completing the www.myuse.org website because we believe in the importance of the message and hope that many who

read this book will embrace this vision and help us carry forward the mission of
My Use International.

Preface

My 20 years of business experience as an owner has taught me that the daily known and obvious crises rarely cause severe damage to the business, because we attend to them. The real damage is caused by gradual unnoticed changes that continue and build up over time, and then, when they are discovered, it is too late to avoid disaster. Such insidious stresses are mounting in the international arena, while we are distracted by day to day crises such as the war on drugs, corporate executive scandals, and celebrity trials.

What qualifies me to talk about these stresses is that I have lived the American experience to the fullest for the past 35 years, replete with worldwide travel, raising a family, and maintaining a successful business, but I was born, raised and educated in a third-world country. Therefore, I can see things that an American-born cannot.

The current reality is that technologies in transportation and communication have forced widely varying cultures into bed together. The East is meeting the West, and the picture will not be pretty in a relatively short time. Trade between nations lulls us into a false sense of comfort. Revolutions in the sciences of physics and genetics could pit the closest allies against each other overnight.

Based on my worldview, World War III between nations is likely within decades. It can be avoided, but the window of opportunity to avert it is narrow. Urgent orientation and controlled changes are needed to avert war between the East and the West. While, we as a society, are concerned by the terrorist-created instability of the world, a much greater crisis, hidden in the folds of this instability, is being overlooked.

From Plato's *Republic* (300-plus BC) to Adam Smith's *The Wealth of Nations* (1776 AD), from Alexis de Toqueville's *Democracy in America* (1835) to *Habits of the Heart: Individualism and Commitment in American Life* (1985), mankind has anticipated the day when governments of the world grow into each other or face annihilation.

A new day is dawning upon those who are awake to it. We are living in an age of hijacked planes, hijacked operating systems, hijacked ideas, and even hijacked nations. The world we inhabit together has changed in fundamental ways. The human race has two choices: ignore all the signs and hope for the best, or accept

the responsibility we bear to ourselves and our descendants. Rising to this responsibility will require nothing short of fresh thinking about the world we live in and
how, as individuals, we can organize and influence it—now. Business as usual is
not an option.

The relevance of all political parties worldwide is under threat. The economic
power of multinational businesses is currently overtaking the power of nation-
states of the world. This is a natural and organic growth of human culture in its
broadest sense; yet as this inevitable change continues unmanaged and unnoticed,
it will result in unprecedented international stress. That stress could very likely be
expressed as WWIII, which could create a nuclear winter that will change the
worldwide human condition as we know it.

In his book, *The Compassionate Conservative* (1996), Dr. Joseph Jacobs argues
that words can tyrannize as much as action. American tyranny (commonly called
imperialism), real or perceived, has narrowed the window of opportunity for
avoiding WWIII. With the pre-emptive attack on Iraq, the world now sees America as another Israel; prone to paranoid thinking and pre-emptive strikes. The victim mentality will only perpetuate the problems of the human race. These types
of activities narrow the window by encouraging negative reactions.

There is a great deal of talk in America about converting crises into opportunities. Yet the opportunity after September 11, 2001 to reflect upon America's foreign policies, which may have flushed out the root causes of that terrorist attack,
has largely gone to waste. After three months of unprecedented reflective thought
in America about our collective safety, we went back to politics as usual.

M. Scott Peck, author of *The Road Less Traveled, The Different Drum* and *People of the Lie: The Hope for Healing Human Evil*, saw in 1987 the characteristics of
a path heading toward WWIII. He said, "Those who cannot think of the future
in terms other than an extrapolation from the status quo will probably think:
'Impractical.' But we must return to the reality that the status quo is murderous."

As WWI and WWII started with conflicts in the second world, WWIII is
likely to start in the third world. The coming clash of political economies is
avoidable, if we choose to be proactive. America has the stature to lead, but needs
the neutrality and credibility to be heard.

Professional politicians must think outside the box, and the baby boomers
must fulfill the dream of their parents, which was to make love, not war. By creating political parties of mankind rather than nations and joining hands on a plat-
form built by the engineering community of the world, there is still hope for us.
The widely respected journalist, George Will says, "America has an engineering

gene in its DNA; we think that where there is a problem there must also be a solution waiting to be found."

What's wrong with that, I'd like to know!

I. Khan

PART I

ORIENTATION
to the concepts forming
the basis for this book.

I like to believe that people in the long run are going to do more to promote peace than our governments. Indeed, I think that people want peace so much that one of these days governments had better get out of the way and let them have it.

—Dwight D. Eisenhower, 34th President of the United States

1

Worldviews

The primary problems of life in America are a shortage of time and a lack of community. This is natural for a country that proudly states, "…the chief business of the American people is business…" (Calvin Coolidge, President of the Untied States, 1923–1929). Business is a game of differentiation. Life is a game of integration. The two do not mix well.

Yet the potential to create an interface between commerce and community is inherent in every one of us.

This possibility exists because how we interpret the world is unique to each individual. My worldview may differ from yours. Here's a simple example:

A woman walks up the aisle, past a seated man on a steady-speed, non-turbulent airplane. She is in a state of motion and he is in a state of rest. To a child on the ground, they are both in a state of motion of a different kind. All Laws of Nature (invoked by the American *Declaration of Independence*) work equally well on the plane as well as on the ground. Therefore, there is no reason to prefer the child's worldview to the man's.

And yet, the child's worldview, seen from a distance, is wider and more inclusive. The only way for either the man or the woman to have a wider worldview is to look outside the window. That is Galileo's theory of relativity. Albert Einstein used this theory to explain the constancy of the speed of light. I am attempting to apply it to physics, philosophy, politics and psychology.

The shared perceptions of a group are the pillars of its reality. Most groups of humans rarely recognize that the "extended sharing of reality" hardens into "righteousness" and that the shared—and righteously agreed upon—ideas of a group are the pillars of its destiny. Time honored beliefs convince a group of people that their way of life is the best way, and that whoever interferes with it is either wrong or bad. Groups can be religious affiliations, nations, businesses, or other associations or organizations of people.

The misunderstandings of groups rapidly become righteous positions, and the result is the death and destruction wrought by war.

◆   ◆   ◆

I believe the most common cognitive distortion is psychological projection, which means assuming that others think, believe and feel the way we do. The misunderstandings created by psychological projection cause fights, whether it is between husband and wife, between groups, or between nations.

You have a right to your worldview. Our constantly widening worldviews are frames of reference out of which our souls navigate our bodies' journeys through time. Every day, in our own little way, we are changing the destiny of mankind through choices with respect to time and money. Our souls gain individual strength by staying in the now, saying no, and knowing what is going on. We gain collective strength through faith and unity. In America, we maintain an integrating attitude in a busy nation, a nation that mostly respects differentiation.

We have grasped the mystery of the atom and rejected the Sermon on the Mount. Ours is a world of nuclear giants and ethical infants. We know more about killing than we do about living.

—Omar Bradley, American General, WWII

2

Safety

Money orchestrates the dance of life, which the law choreographs. Over the last century, power struggles have caused two World Wars, and still today humanity remains oblivious to three realities:

1. Power struggles are a losing proposition, for *wars won are costlier than wars lost.*

2. Economic expansion is on the rise, and undetected stress is gradually building towards a potential third World War, which is brewing between the entrenched ways of the West and the expanding power of the East.

3. True safety does not come from walls, defensive weapons, or money; it comes from good relationships.

People choose to impose order upon their own lives to reap the benefits of the social contract, and then go on to complain about it anyway. We must stop operating from a victim mentality. As soon as a person stands responsible in the moment, his or her thought shifts to the future and life becomes more pleasant.

Every one of us tries to get away with as much as we can. That's human nature. But, we must resist the urge to be shortsighted. Immediate goals should not be given priority over long-term vision, as seems to be the way of life at the beginning of the 21st century.

◆　　◆　　◆

In his 1776 book, *The Wealth of Nations,* Adam Smith astutely noted that he has never observed a dog trade a bone with another dog. Man is the only animal capable of barter and trade. Smith went on to explain how money is useful in facilitating trade, and how unregulated markets are the most efficient, because they are regulated by nature. He noted that growing economies yield higher wages than richer ones. He drew attention to the higher wages and lower cost of living in America compared to England. No wonder America declared independence.

Because man has progressed, it is appropriate to shift concern from wealth to health, hence the title of this book, *The Health of Nations*. It addresses physical safety problems of the kind caused by nuclear explosions, and mental health problems of the kind caused by civilization.

No other animal but man puts away his own kind (behind bars and out of sight) for the protection and safety of the ordinary citizen. Man's focus on self-preservation leads to delusional fascination with possessions of security. Man is so busy conducting trade that he has forgotten how to live. Society assists the conformed man and rewards him by "protecting his just right to property." The ripple effect on others goes untracked. But its result shows up. Jails are full of criminals that lived in too much defiance, and insane asylums are full of people who lived in too much compliance.

Only seers watch reality in a cross-generational sense. Terrorists attack international monuments of trade, and the human race has placed collective suicide within its own reach.

◆   ◆   ◆

Why would a sane person want to risk his time, money, energy, and even credibility on the issue of WWIII? It is simply a matter of priorities.

My life, like that of most people, used to be rushed; it was missing that element life is truly made of—time. Ever since I learned to separate urgency from importance, most deadlines lost their meaning, and life worked better—both at work and at home. The following is my progression of priorities.

1. Food and water

2. Shelter

3. Safety

4. Health and fitness

5. Discipline

    a. Delaying Gratification (patience)

    b. Not operating from the victim mentality (taking responsibility)

    c.   Dedication to Reality (ever widening worldviews)

    d.   Balancing (too much of anything is bad)

6.   Love (the will to help each other and to be a positive influence)

7.   Worldview (respecting everyone's worldview)

8.   Grace (truly accepting life and death)

Nature's God blessed me with all of the above. My family and employees are also taken care of, although I jump into problems of safety when my children drive too fast, or my employees work too hard. Having covered all those fronts, I chose to work on the next problem of safety: planetary safety.

◆   ◆   ◆

America is a great country. But it does not have perspective on itself. No entity does. Therefore, we must use our wits to help America.

We can make our lives less stressful if the world is a safer place. The last great concept was the *Constitution of the United States of America*, but politicians have abused their power within it since about 1930. The world is ready for the next great synergy. We can make the next synthesis diplomatic, through foresight and diplomacy, or allow it to become violent, through myopia and hypocrisy.

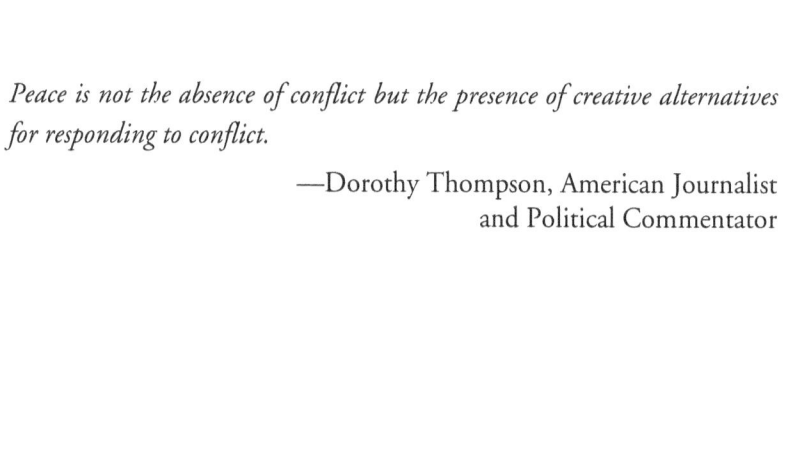

Peace is not the absence of conflict but the presence of creative alternatives for responding to conflict.

—Dorothy Thompson, American Journalist
and Political Commentator

3

Conflict

In 1982, I toured Europe for two weeks by car with a gentleman named Gulzar, who was well versed in political science. I drove and he talked, filling me in on world history. I found his narrative and depth fascinating. At one point, I asked him about the causes of WWI and WWII. After giving me some specific incidents, he said, "Wars are caused by economic conflict." I started laughing and replied, "That sounds like an irresponsible cop-out by the victorious theocrats, monarchs, aristocrats or democrats."

Even if true, saying, "Wars between nations are caused by economic conflict," is like saying, "Accidents between cars are caused by metallic conflict." The real cause, in my opinion, is that the leaders of nations lacked the vision to see a conflict coming up in the future and therefore could not take measures to avert it. After a war, why should they say, "It was my fault?"

◆   ◆   ◆

There is more logic behind my opinion, which I'd like to communicate by telling a personal story. When I was ten years old, my father was involved with the governance of remote, sparsely populated areas in the Karakoram Range of the Himalayan Mountains. There were small deltaic deposits of soil at the estuary of each mountain stream. The terrain was so rugged that people cultivated crops in narrow-stepped fields. Due to difficulty in travel, there was little exchange between communities, and different languages were often spoken from village to village.

I learned *Sheena*, the language of the capital. The language in Jutial, about five miles away, was difficult to comprehend. The language in Chhamoogarh was totally different. The language in Hunza, a famous location because of the length (at that time) of the life span of its residents, was incomprehensible.

After my father supervised the construction of dirt roads, which were navigated by jeeps, the natural result was increased trade. In the process of conducting trade, people would engage each other in idle chatter with no recognition of the problem such conversations could create. Having lived within their generational cocoons of beliefs and imprisoned in the nuances of their own native languages, they did not realize that their worldviews were different and that they could easily show disrespect without intending it.

The trade increased communication, which resulted in misunderstandings, stress and strife. Skirmishes gradually became more and more violent. As the overseer of all this, my father remained neutral towards them, with no loyalties to either side. I noticed the impact of improved transportation on the state of conflict between humans. The government should have anticipated the problems, and held orientation sessions before introducing jeep roads.

Winds of change swept across that microcosm as winds of change are now sweeping across the globe. The reason then was underestimating the stress of technological progress (dirt roads). The reason now is underestimating the stress of technological progress (airplane travel and the Internet information superhighway) and corporate globalization.

◆   ◆   ◆

In my teenage years, I asked myself why two world wars happened in this one century and none ever before. Based on the microcosm I had experienced (described above), I concluded that world wars became possible because of improved means of naval and aerial transportation. Had the visionary leaders of nations been aware of the price of transportation improvements, they might have added a new facet to their diplomacy.

As an example, the book *A Century of War* by F. William Engdahl published in 1993 and summarized in Alan Jones' *How the World Really Works*, explains that Germany was building a railroad from Baghdad to Berlin to have access to Middle East oil fields, bypassing sea routes controlled by the British. Because the world's war machinery is dependent upon petroleum for fuel, Great Britain's strategy several decades prior to World War I was to secure its strength by controlling this raw material.

Before the last link to the railroad in Serbia could be finished, the Austrian heir-apparent was assassinated by a Serb, to which Austria responded by bringing in Germany, France (and Britain by sub-treaty to France), and Russia, by treaty with either Serbia or Austria, thereby starting the First World War. Germany was successfully cut off from both Russian and Middle-Eastern oil and the war was essentially won with Rockefeller oil from America.

Britain had viewed Germany's economic strengthening in the early 1900s with alarm. Had the nations involved foreseen how belief systems exacerbate the conflict caused by competing economic expansions, they may have held orientation programs for themselves and others decades before the war broke out, at a time when the distrust was not so high. Or they could have asked a third party, such as America, to mediate. The power struggle to "gain mastery" would have lost some of its zeal, and compromises could have happened without all-out war.

Nowadays, technologies of transportation and communication are driving the world. The information superhighway reminds me of the roads in the Himalayan Mountains. Because it creates great benefit, we tend to forget that it also could have a devastating side effect.

◆   ◆   ◆

In April 1991, I found a unique and personal way to approach the problem. I visualized an imaginary place on the moon from which I could observe all of the earth. For the past 12 years, I have mentally retreated there to relax and watch the whitish blue globe, with detachment, with one purpose in mind: to understand what is going on among the members of the human race, so that I can help in a leveraged way.

Once I reached a high degree of clarity about our deepest problems, I knew it was time to act, to share my views about how we can create permanent world peace, as well as lasting inner peace.

◆   ◆   ◆

Wars "in our own backyards" have a way of knocking sense into the collective minds of the human race. It took the War of Independence to create the American *Constitution*. It took WWI to get the League of Nations going. It took WWII to form the United Nations. The fall of the Soviet Union lulled everyone into a false sense of complacency.

Only the people on this planet, own this planet, and we each have a responsibility toward planetary stewardship. We must recognize and choose to honor this task, individually and collectively, or face WWIII.

Will it take a third world war, a nuclear war, to knock some sense into us?

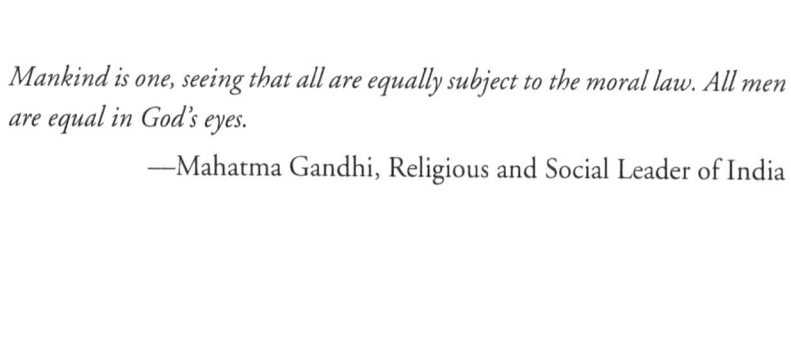

Mankind is one, seeing that all are equally subject to the moral law. All men are equal in God's eyes.

—Mahatma Gandhi, Religious and Social Leader of India

4

Laws

I am no scholar of law, yet the following could help us gain perspective on the legal struggles of modern man.

Laws are rules. Their interplay with facts determines the course of action in the court of civilization. No system of law is useful unless society has the resources to evaluate both its interplay with the facts of the day and the values that society holds dear, and the will to enforce it.

The following is a rough chronology of legal systems. While I am unwilling to argue whether these are God's laws or man's laws, I will be writing about them as if they were man's laws. See if you can spot the emerging pattern.

About 2100 B.C.: Abraham's concept of one God is his first attempt to bring coordination and mental health to this planet.

About 1400 B.C.: Moses' *Ten Commandments* takes the matter one step further by outlining clear definitions of acceptable behavior.

About 350 B.C.: Aristotle says, "Law is reason devoid of passion." Perhaps he is compelled to say this because he can see profit-driven absurdities in the Greek legal system.

When Jesus is born in 1 A.D., the Jewish people are into their fourth millennium. Jesus finds them to be over-regulated and tied by their own laws into knots of frustration and inaction. He says that they should just love each other, and relax about the strict application of the law. (I am guessing that profit-related absurdities had grown to intolerable levels in Jerusalem by then, and a revolution was needed.) Naturally, the scholars and lawmakers (the establishment), who have vested their whole lives into the learning and application of the system, are threatened; thus, Jesus meets an unjust and untimely death.

About 600 A.D., Mohammad learns of the Judeo-Christian tradition during his business trips and establishes a direct genealogical connection with Abraham, through Abraham's second son, Ishmael. An analysis of the daily Muslim prayer clearly illustrates that Mohammad feels Abraham's one-God concept needs rein-forcement. Thus, he proclaims the equality of all humans.

The same prayer also implies that he feels the Jewish people lean too much towards prosperity (and security) and the Christian people lean too much towards peace. He aims for both peace and prosperity in the daily Muslim prayer. To prevent people from straying away from the path of Abraham in the future, he proclaims himself the last prophet, and the *Qur'an*, the last holy book. In the *Qur'an*, he adds many rules of state (laws of man). These laws are called *sharia*, and like most other legal systems today are outdated, even though Muslim clerics still derive legitimacy (and livelihoods) from them. Most Muslim countries are still practicing these laws, and they continue to make the mistake of mixing mosque and state.

A realization of the Indian civilization is that, "Law is blind." I believe this means blind with respect to emotion, thus validating Aristotle's observation.

By 18th century A.D., Galileo, Newton, Martin Luther and Queen Elizabeth I usher in the Age of Reason in the West, which brings about the advent of man's law and, at least in the West, the separation of church and state.

Napoleon creates the Western system of law from the concept of "fairness." This system becomes over-regulated in England. Over-application of archaic laws leads to a jail population that cannot be supported by society. Therefore, England is forced to export its prisoners to Australia, a practice that endures for 62 years.

The U.S. *Declaration of Independence* invokes the Laws of Nature and Nature's God when declaring the American colonies separate and independent from England:

> *When in the Course of human events, it becomes necessary for one people to dissolve the political bands which have connected them with another, and to assume among the powers of the earth, the separate and equal station to which the Laws of Nature and of Nature's God entitle them, a decent respect to the opinions of mankind requires that they should declare the causes which impel them to the separation.*

In the second paragraph of this important document, our Founding Fathers claimed, as a Law of Nature and of Nature's God, "certain inalienable Rights," among which are Life, Liberty and the pursuit of Happiness, and—although it took more than two more centuries to accomplish—Equality. The declaration goes on to say, "Whenever any Form of Government becomes destructive to these ends, it is the Right of the People to alter or to abolish it, and to institute new Government, laying its foundation on such principles and organizing its powers in such form, as to them shall seem most likely to effect their Safety and

Happiness." The Founding Fathers went on to write the *Constitution of the United States*, which was a successful attempt to make sense of the reality that was current then. In Chapter 2, I referred to the *U.S. Constitution* as THE LAST GREAT CONCEPT.

As we have seen, historically, such systems of law—however well-meaning—become obsolete. Thomas Jefferson argued for a complete rewrite every 20 years, for he felt corrupt politicians would hijack the amendment process. He was right. Current U.S. law has doubled the jail population from one million to over two million in the last ten years, and profit-related absurdities are on the rise.

A good example of such absurdity is the way television networks are acting as How-To Manuals for terrorists by describing which borders are insecure, etc. And take Tom Clancy's works of fiction, *Debt of Honor* (1994) and *Executive Orders* (1996), which with their uncanny description of the events leading up to September 11, 2001, anticipated the reality that was to come. *Debt of Honor* ended with a passenger plane crashing into a Capitol building, and *Executive Orders* started with the threat of an Ebola virus being unleashed on the country.

The intent of law is results; yet, it must rely on due process for it to be self-consistent on the topic of fairness. The practice of law with due process becomes (with the passage of time) so extensive that even the lawyers do not know it all. Thus, they have to research it, or go to "specialty" lawyers. When this happens, society is expressing its need for a from-the-ground-up reform in the form of THE NEXT GREAT CONCEPT.

"Fairness is in the eye of the beholder," proclaims Dr. Joseph Jacobs in his 1996 book, *The Compassionate Conservative*. Herein lies the threat to the legitimacy and the stability of Western law.

◆   ◆   ◆

If you want corn, you must plant the seeds of corn. Laws of Nature cannot be violated, even if we wish to violate them. Thus they are self-enforced.

Laws of life are the natural social rules that govern the interaction of mankind. They exist much like the Laws of nature, and are automatically enforced.

These laws are well documented by Dr. Philip McGraw (Dr. Phil) in his 1999 book, *Life Strategies*, in which he says, "Our world is like an unguided missile; all speed, no control." He adds, "This nation is losing it." I believe he is talking about the mental health of America.

Peace is not the product of terror or fear. Peace is not the silence of cemeteries. Peace is not the silent result of violent repression. Peace is the generous, tranquil contribution of all to the good of all.

—Oscar Romero, El Salvador Archbishop
and Martyr for the Poor

5

Principles of Cohabitation

The real order of our future world will likely be imposed on the world community by rapidly advancing technologies of transportation and communication. This world order will be created around the concepts of Abrahamic and Eastern traditions (trade conditions). The collective political will of mankind will determine the future world order.

How well will we live together in this future? Our comfortable peaceful cohabitation in the world depends on a few principles we learn as we grow up, and mold, as we mature.

Trust

I have a bad habit of extending my trust too quickly to too many people. And yet, when sitting at my computer, I cannot get myself to click, "trust Microsoft," or even to send an error report to Microsoft. How can I trust such a giant corporation that nearly monopolizes the world's computer operating systems?

As I hasten to click on the "I Accept" legal mumbo jumbo about software and the Internet, I know that I am compromising myself for the sake of expediency. Most probably you are doing the same. And yet, I must have faith in "others," for "they" (including Microsoft) have brought me to where I am, which is happy and successful. Still, I do not trust Microsoft because I've heard that it is not happy with only controlling the world's computer operating systems. Now it's rumored that that corporation is busy buying out the rights to good books, which may lead to control of reading material.

I will never trust an entity that wants to be the gatekeeper of my mind.

Respect

I believe that lasting peace comes from mutual respect.

The best leader—ever—of my birth country, Pakistan, lived many decades ago. His name was Ayub Khan (no relation) and he wrote a book called, *Friends, Not Masters*. He has my respect, even though we never met. It is not only possible, but also important, that we learn enough about each other to have the opportunity for respect.

Our actions are our ethics.

Our appreciations are our aesthetics.

Love

I define love as the will of the divine. It expresses itself in the gravity of the earth and the light of the sun. It interacts with the universe, creating bodies of life, which convert energy into matter (cells) and matter (food) into energy. Its force transcends the forces of economics described by Karl Marx and Adam Smith.

There are many words used to describe love in India, including *pyaar, muhabbat, chaahat* and *ulfat*. The word *ishq* describes the highest intensity and is a good description of divine love. The word *vehshat* describes a degree of love that borders on insanity. The poet Ghalib lived over 150 years ago, and in his verse he wrote that mankind would celebrate him centuries after his death, because ultimately, we would catch on to his poetry. Jean Jacques Rousseau of France wrote *The Social Contract* in 1762. His *vehshsat* brought about the reign of terror in France 30 years later. It is now resonating worldwide. So who is insane?

India has been talking of non-violence and love for centuries. It must be totally and utterly disappointed in the half-witted actions of mankind. The word for such disappointment is, *"mayoos."*

Division of Labor

The division of labor brings out the best in people, but it can also, on occasion, confuse us into poor judgment. For example, man started practicing bad psychology around the time of Joseph (when the storage of food allowed more free time), which was the dawn of civilization in Mesopotamia about 10,000 years ago. The excess time led to reflective thinking, which then created the concept of insanity and led to regulation of sin by the Ten Commandments. I like the latter, but the former is not good.

Back then, trepanning was a popular practice among the Mesopotamians as a cure for insanity (non-conformity?). It was done by drilling a hole in the skull through the patient's temple, to relieve pressure from the mind. To me, it sounds like society started passing judgment when it could not understand the motivation of a man's actions.

The summary of my reflective thinking is that:

- Religions are competing for our hearts. Let that be, as long as they do not mess with our minds.

- Nations are competing for our minds. Let that be, as long as they do not mess with our money.

- Businesses are competing for our money. Let that be, as long as the playing field is level.

Who should decide whether the playground is level? That is where the NEXT GREAT CONCEPT comes in.

Each time a man stands up for an ideal, or acts to improve the lot of others, or strikes out against injustice, he sends forth a tiny ripple of hope, and crossing each other from a million different centers of energy and daring, those ripples build a current that can sweep down the mightiest walls of oppression and resistance.

—Robert Kennedy, former U.S. Senator and Attorney General

6

Become Aware

In *The Seven Habits of Highly Effective People* (Stephen R. Covey, 1990), the first habit is, Being Proactive. I want to be proactive on behalf of the human race. What follows will assist you not only in assessing the dangers of the next decade or two, it will also create opportunities for you to create inner peace by focusing on world peace. It may even aid you with personal prosperity by helping you to understand our world as it is now, and its apparent direction, so that you can best navigate your own life accordingly.

Mainland China chose its independence day to coincide with the first day of the American government's fiscal year (October 1). Taiwan's Independence Day is October 10. The economic heartbeat of the world resonates from China to America. China's independence came in 1949. The dawn of the information age occurred shortly after two nuclear bombs were dropped on Japan, near the end of World War II. Information was defined in 1990 as, "That which reduces uncertainty," by *Positioning* authors Al Ries and Jack Trout.

A new day has dawned upon those who are awake to it. Even as the widely respected magazine, *Foreign Affairs*, continues to be produced, the situation of this world now lends itself to renaming the magazine *Internal Affairs* because global affairs affect us quite internally.

It took Japan a long time to come to grips with the reality of the nuclear bomb, even though the evidence was clear. The human race is now confronted with a similar uncomfortable reality. Unfortunately, the evidence is not as clear as the bombs on Japan. This book identifies the indications of a pending World War III.

On the time scale of history, WWIII between the East and the West is imminent. It is likely to be a war that will employ wanton use of nuclear weaponry, because death and destruction has rarely been a deterrent to man. The good news is that the war can be avoided, and that you can be part of the solution instead of being part of the problem.

Humanity moves forward in the cradles of great concepts, such as the *U.S. Constitution*. Some concepts give rise to new technologies, which make the original concept un-amendable and obsolete. Beyond the United States, it is time for an inclusive, great, WORLDWIDE NEW CONCEPT. The challenge is to create an approach that will bring a worldwide new concept gradually and with responsibility, with love and respect, so that the disenchanted peoples of the world see a timetable for their salvation, and WWIII is prevented.

This book presents such an approach. The intent is to make the synthesis intellectual and diplomatic, for we have time to make it happen. Otherwise, with our heads buried in the sand like frightened ostriches, we are headed for catastrophe. I can but pray that I am wrong.

I was born, raised and educated on the other side of the globe. I can see things about America that American-born citizens cannot see. I have "perspective" on America. What is perspective? A fish swimming in water does not have perspective on water. Think of me as a person who lived in air for about 21 years and then lived in water with the rest of America for about 35 years.

As a first-generation American, my views are more global compared to someone born in America. This planet is of the people, by the people, for the people. And yet, all political parties of all nations are under threat of gradual extinction, even without a nuclear war. The state of affairs of the human race is currently transitioning from dominance by nation-states to dominance by multi-national corporations. As of 2001, fifty-one of the top one hundred economies in the world are businesses, and forty-nine are nation-states. This trend will likely continue; but if we are to transition successfully, we must adapt by innovation. It is the author's considered opinion that the next adaptation of the human race requires the creation of many new political parties, each representing humanity, rather than a given nation. More on my effort toward this end in Chapter 16.

PART II

EXPLANATION
of the reasoning toward my
conclusions.

If we want world peace, we must let go of our attachments and truly live like nomads. That's where I no mad at you, you no mad at me. That way, there'll surely be no madness on the planet. And peace begins with each of us. A little peace here, a little peace there, pretty soon all the peaces will fit together to make one big peace everywhere.

—Swami Beyondananda, American Humorist

7

Realizations and Civilizations

Buddha's central realization, "Life is suffering," is a great insight. Over two thousand years later, author M. Scott Peck proclaimed, "Life is difficult." Apparently, it has improved from "suffering" to "difficult." Yet, Benjamin Franklin treated life like a toy, tinkering with it, to see how he could better enjoy it to his own endless amusement.

◆   ◆   ◆

A primary realization of mine is that humor is one of the most important stepping-stones on the road to peace. Let me share a few apparently unrelated concepts, and then connect the dots to illustrate the broader picture.

As a teenager in a third world country, I was always puzzled by the section called, "Laughter, the Best Medicine" in *Reader's Digest*. What was so funny about that? All of my friends were equally baffled, for they also saw absolutely nothing humorous in those jokes. Often, we would find the punch line cruel rather than funny. I even remember wondering whether I somehow misunderstood the meaning of the title, "Laughter, the Best Medicine."

Then I happened to run across a British book titled, *American Humor*. What compelled an apparently sane person to labor over this topic? Obviously, he was trying to help his fellow Britons get a grasp on that which is funny in American humor. So it became clear to me that I had correctly understood the meaning behind the words, "laughter, the best medicine." It was the content of the humor that I was misunderstanding. I suspect that even the British, who share the same language and heritage with America, have to stretch in order to "get it." Even though the cultures and language are similar, the humor is quite different. Imagine how much greater is the difference in humor between less similar cultures.

I remember a joke I used to find funny while I was still in Pakistan. The setup was, "Why are you crying?" The punch line was, "I am not crying, this is my natural look." It does not sound funny any more. Life is different in America—America is not suffering like the third world, that's why. Having lived in America for 35 years, I now understand American humor.

The point is that if we can understand another people's humor, we have a good chance of understanding what is important to them as well. And we must keep our sense of humor as we work together for world peace. Many of us would like to change the world, but we are too busy to even begin to change ourselves. This keeps the world a serious place.

Former President Ronald Reagan was a master of good humor, which had its place in politics. During his first presidential campaign in 1980, Reagan was 68 years old, and his age was a highly sensitive issue. During his debate with Walter Mondale, everyone was on edge wondering if Mondale would paint Reagan as too old for the office. Before Mondale said anything, Reagan beat him to the punch and said something like, "Let's not bring up the issue of age, for I do not want the youth and inexperience of my opponent to weigh in against him."

And the good humor of Reagan and former Soviet leader Mikhail Gorbachev was evident to anyone who watched them on television. They effectively ended the Cold War. One television exchange between them still makes me smile on the inside. For the benefit of the cameras, Reagan had just uttered the Russian proverb, "Trust but verify" one too many times. Instead of taking offense, Gorbachev good-naturedly extended his hand and delivered the following punch line with a beaming face, "Why is it, Mr. President, that every time we meet, you bring this up?" Everyone cracked up. That is the way to live.

◆   ◆   ◆

A second realization came to me in 1991: either you get it, or you don't. Later, in 1999, Dr. Phil published it in his book, *Life strategies*. The point of the book was that in any given situation, there is a governing factor. Those who get it, do well; those who don't, do poorly.

Elbert Hubbard, prolific American writer, printer and lecturer in the early 1900s, says that the best way to live life is to view it as a game. Those who "get it" know this option. The tools of the game are actions, looks, words and numbers. The purpose of the game is different in the West. In the West, the purpose is to accumulate maximum value for yourself, and the "invisible hand" of Adam Smith (British philosopher and economist in the 1700s) will produce maximum value for society naturally. Those who are left out due to inability will be taken care of by charity. In the East, where I was born and raised, the purpose of the game is to please God and be resigned to fate. The point is that the governing factor of the game of life is different in different cultures.

India got the concept of non-violence millennia earlier. To practice that, in 1994, I hired an airplane to fly over Nixon's funeral in Yorba Linda with a message which read, "Non-Violence; Starting Now." The authorities ran the airplane off. Perhaps they thought I was implying that Nixon was a symbol of war.

Just as it takes two to fight, it takes two to make peace. India has been invaded over and over again by stupid warriors and finally driven to a point where it has assumed the name, "*Bharat*" and decided to fight back. Is anybody paying attention? No, we still call the country India and we do not stop to look and listen to the meaning behind the word *Bharat,* which was the name of a warrior king. The symbolism for "we are tired of non-violence and being pushed around" is clear.

If one of the more loving civilizations of the world was reduced to violence, then who am I to hope differently? Well, there is a saying from that civilization: "The world is stable due to hope." *Pay attention please.* I repeat, "The world is stable due to hope." And I hope we "get it" that the governing factor in obtaining world peace is non-violence. Mahatma Gandhi of India got it, and Martin Luther King, Jr. of the U.S. got it, to name a few well known examples.

◆　　◆　　◆

My third realization is regarding America's arrogance about democracy. Love overcomes arrogance and ignorance, but only if it is attended to. The world perceives America as arrogant, a country that thinks its way of life will work everywhere. I may be ignorant, but I am on the world's side on this one. I was born, raised and educated in a third world country (Pakistan) that has tried democracy many times in its history. Every single time, the experiment in democracy failed, as it did in Greece during the times of Plato. It brought the country close to anarchy, and the army had to step in as dictator to maintain order. Everyone breathed a huge sigh of relief, but as soon as stability was established, the people started attacking the very leaders who saved them, and the march towards democracy started again.

Pakistan is torn between its absolute faith in Adam's God, and the shining democracy called America. Hardly anyone knows that America is not a democracy. It is a republic. They are similar in that people are free and have an equal right to participate in government. In a republic, participation is indirect in that people elect representatives who are given the power to speak and vote for them.

If we cannot pay attention to the name, *Bharat,* which shows up as an error in Microsoft Word, who can be blamed for such ignorance about what works?

Envy and loathing are the feelings that best describe the world's view of America. If they only knew the burden of leadership we carry! All the while, America perceives the world as ignorant, for it "knows" that democracy and free market capitalism (which collapsed in 1929—and the Federal Reserve's bandage is beginning to come off now) are the ways to a great life. However, America's generosity is stretched, fear is on the rise, and hearts are hardening every day, even though everyone is doing the best they can with what they have. No wonder it is said, "The road to hell is paved with good intentions."

Somehow, America conveniently forgets about its own most powerful concept, separation of church and state. That is one of the principles upon which this country was founded. The *Declaration of Independence* invoked Nature's God.

I will say only two words to America, and even those are borrowed from Dr. Phil: "Get real." Or I might remind America of the words of the Duke of Wellington, who allowed us all to speak English by defeating Napoleon. He said, "Wars won are costlier than wars lost."

After winning the Cold War, we should have dug our heels in for a long hard time, to win Jimmy Carter's often berated "moral equivalent of war," instead of stepping into the hornet's nest of the Middle East. And if you think the Middle East is a problem, you ain't seen nothin' yet.

Should we manage to avoid WWIII, America (280 million people) is headed towards becoming to Islam (1.3 billion people) as Israel is to Palestine. Meanwhile, I marvel at the competence of the Jewish people who are in the year 5764, for even though there are only 14 million of them, they dominate the attention of the world.

My friends and relatives flying back and forth from Pakistan and India tell me the people over there hate America, especially after the Iraq attack. Yet everyone is copying American ways in regard to music, clothing, conversation and fast food.

Isn't imitation the sincerest form of flattery? It seems to me that the world is in a love/hate relationship with America. But then, people are often in love/hate relationships with leaders. They become envious of the privileges of leadership, yet they remain ignorant of the burdens.

Arrogance is the quality that demoted Lucifer from God's favorite to the hated Satan. Ignorance is the one quality Mohammad hated. Yet one man's ignorance is another man's arrogance. We have a tendency to become too married to our ideas and beliefs. After a while we just "know" what we know. Any social psychologist will attest to that. Shakespeare, who is still selling more books than any author (Bible excepted) said, "Nothing is good or bad, only thinking makes it so." The Persian poet Sufi Rumi said, "Out beyond ideas of wrong doing and right doing, there's a field. I'll meet you there." He must be quite lonely.

I have nothing against right, wrong, rules, regulations, morality, ethics etc., but these things differ greatly in different countries. The biggest differences are between the East and the West. This is why the British realization, "East is East, and West is West, and never the twain shall meet,…" is profound.

◆   ◆   ◆

Finally, an ancient Chinese proverb proclaims, "I hear, I forget; I see, I remember; I do, I understand." Socrates said, "We observe with our eyes and we understand with our souls." So what does this have to do with the world situation? And what was my final realization?

It is that the human race is incapable of understanding each other across nations in general, especially across the East and the West, for one nation/civilization has not walked in the shoes of another. The nations have fought wars side-by-side and against each other, yet worldviews remain different. We live under the illusion that one country can reason with another. Yet, serious reasoning always emanates from that entity's worldview, so this is simply not possible.

Let me spell it out in relation to humor. How are most jokes told? A typical joke starts with a description of an everyday situation. A good joke teller will take his time, describing the everyday situation, providing visual imagery to prepare the listener's mind in a routine context. In most good jokes, the punch line accomplishes two purposes. First, it changes the context. But for the joke to get a belly laugh, the new context must refer to insights gained by the audience through common experience, preferably taboo from daily conversation for ethical reasons.

The latter point reminds us all of the fact that we are all imperfect, struggling through life facing somewhat similar challenges. We don't talk about these things much, for there is not time enough. The hint of a deeply shared insight produces the delight of spiritual union. And we all laugh together, for we feel the joy of communing, and the disappearance of being alone.

We know in that moment that life is a challenge for all of us, and we are all trying our best to cope with it. Those having similar experiences are running into similar challenges, for man is not only political by nature, he is also governed by economics.

The Americans and the British have had different experiences of life, so it is hard to grasp the underlying commonality of understanding. The same applies to different parts of the world, but to a much higher degree. Even the French commitment to liberty of spirit, in the face of "the business of life", is lost upon Americans.

There has been no shared experience between the East and the West upon which to build a common ground of understanding. While England understands India (as is obvious from British movies like *Gandhi* and *A Passage to India*), I have yet to see one American movie made in India that captures the essence of India.

How will the East and the West live together in the 21st century, if we do not understand each other? And yet we are now in bed, thrown together by technologies of transportation and communication.

Habit five of *The 7 Habits of Highly Effective People* advises us to "Seek first to understand and then to be understood." Principles of empathic listening are discussed in this book, but there is no discussion of the possibility of our innate inability to understand each other. There is an implicit assumption that given the proper tools, we can understand a shared vision and that anyone can understand without the experience of one's soul.

The "young woman/old woman" experiment from the late twentieth century, where one looks at a picture and either sees a young woman or an old woman depending on his/her experience, clearly illustrates that we will be married to our perspectives, unable to see with the other's eyes. We must have a profound, shared experience for this to occur. Perhaps that experience will begin with an Internet-based political party of mankind, which may lead to the next great concept.

Even after that common experience of having seen the "young woman" or the "old woman," it still takes a long time to truly understand. I used to feel like throwing up when I would eat Western food during my first year in North America, for it was too bland. And Bach and Beethoven sounded like screeches to me for a few years.

Where are you going to find such brutal honesty in today's "politically correct" world? Or should I be saying, "tactful," or even "ethical" world?

We Americans are not capable of understanding the East no matter how hard we try, because people of the East have lived different experiences than people of the West. This great truth is a dangerous one. The human psyche wishes to block it. The reality is too painful. In today's small world, where Japan is the second largest economy, and others like China and India, are catching up fast, there is no Great Wall to protect us from ourselves.

In my view of the world as a family, England is the mother, because she is in psychological control; America is the son who is young, strong and prosperous without much experience; India is the daughter full of feelings about love and emotion; and China is the father, because he is mature, wise, and calm.

China gave us the classic book, *The Art of War*, which suggests the best wars are the ones never fought; the best warrior is the one who is never known after the victory; and the best way to fight is for the war to be over before the opponent realizes a war is underway.

The Chinese say that no matter how hard we try, we cannot understand the other party's point of view, "unless we have walked in their shoes." Even turning the other cheek, which really means viewing the situation from a different angle (in Aramaic), will not do it in today's world. How can one nation walk in the shoes of another nation? Therein lays the challenge.

Everyone is focused on the Middle East. This area is getting sufficient attention. It will not be the place where the problem is totally uncontrollable. Even the Muslims are in the open now, after dialing 911. The slow, unnoticed, silent changes that end up in eruptions are the deadly ones. Trade between nations often lulls us into a false sense of security.

Meanwhile, as a result of gargantuan misunderstandings, we are living in an emotionally polarized world. The world has seen nations born through the specter of terrorism such as Israel and likely Palestine. Are we creating a bad precedent?

And sages of the prophet level are being ignored. Author M. Scott Peck says, "It is not impractical to consider seriously changing the rules of the game if the game is killing us," and, "We must return to the reality that the status quo is murderous." Understanding and acceptance of each other is of utmost importance.

With malice toward none; with charity for all;…let us strive on to finish the work we are in;…to do all which may achieve and cherish a just, and a lasting peace, among ourselves, and with all nations.

—Abraham Lincoln, 16th President of the United States

8

The State of Affairs

The following opening remarks, from *Timeline*, a 2001 novel by Michael Crichton, should cure any sensible person of the illusion that America, the European Union, the United Nations (UN), the World Trade Organization (WTO), the World Bank, the International Monetary Fund (IMF)—or any other entity—will be able to maintain control of the planet without the voluntary cooperation of the vast majority of our nation-states.

A hundred years ago, as the nineteenth century drew to close, scientists around the world were satisfied that they had arrived at a satisfactory picture of the world. As physicist Alastair Rae put it, "By the end of the nineteenth century, it seemed that the basic fundamental principles governing the behavior of the physical universe were known." (Quantum Physics: Illusion or Reality?) Indeed, many scientists said that the study of physics was nearly completed: no big discoveries remained to be made, only details and finishing touches.

But, late in the final decade, a few curiosities came to light. Roentgen discovered rays that passed through flesh; because they were unexplained, he called them X rays. Two months later, Henri Bacquerel accidentally found that a piece of uranium ore emitted something that fogged photographic plates. And the electron, the carrier of electricity, was discovered in 1897.

Yet on the whole, physicists remained calm, expecting that these oddities would eventually be explained by existing theory. No one would have predicted that within five years their complacent view of the world would be shockingly upended, producing an entirely new conception of the universe and entirely new technologies that would transform daily life in the twentieth century in unimaginable ways.

If you were to say to a physicist in 1899 that in 1999, a hundred years later, moving images would be transmitted into homes all over the world from satellites in the sky; that bombs of unimaginable power would threaten the species; that antibiotics would abolish infectious disease but that disease would fight back; that women would have the vote and pills to control reproduction; that millions of people would take to the air every hour in aircraft capable of taking off and landing without human touch; that you could cross the Atlantic at two thousand miles an hour; that human kind would travel to the moon, and then lose interest; that microscopes would be able to see individual atoms; that people could carry telephones weighing a few ounces, and speak anywhere in the world without wires; or that most of these miracles depended on devices the size of a postage stamp, which utilized a new theory called quantum mechanics. If you said all this, the physicist would almost certainly pronounce you mad.

Most of these developments could not have been predicted in 1899, because prevailing scientific theory said they were impossible. And for the few developments that were not impossible such as airplanes, the sheer scale of their eventual use would have defied comprehension. One might have imagined an airplane—but ten thousand airplanes in the air at the same time would have been beyond imagining.

So it is fair to say that even the most informed scientist, standing on the threshold of the twentieth century, had no idea what was to come.

It is also fair to say that even the most informed person, standing on the threshold of the twenty-first century, has no idea of what is to come. Therefore, we can only lay a foundation for the twenty-first century, before building a bridge to it.

No one can say which person or country will be responsible for the next major breakthrough in physics, making the Star Wars defense outdated. Wouldn't it be better to live with respect and humility in this world?

◆   ◆   ◆

The current world situation is unstable and dangerous. Businesses are overtaking nation-states in economic power. Again, let me repeat, as of 2001, 51 out of the world's 100 largest economies were corporations (aristocracies of finance) and 49 were nation-states (many were democracies of opportunity). The power of unelected businessmen is growing beyond the power of elected keepers of the public trust.

Books, documenting the silent and gradual takeover of the world's affairs by big business, are largely written by historians, academicians, politicians, journalists, sociologists, and economists. Most of these books, essays and articles focus on negative consequences because multi-national businesses, even the legendary *kairitsus* (common pools of large businesses to guarantee lifelong employment) of Japan, have proven to be incapable keepers of the public trust. CEOs are responsible to their shareholders, not the homeless and the terrorized of the world.

No solutions have been offered by this slew of books, yet the numbers of organized protests have risen over the last two years. Incidentally, forces of history are inexorably leading towards separation of state and business, as they led to separation of church and state a few centuries ago.

With this in mind, the focus should be on the proper management of this inexorable and innate trend. We saw a need to regulate how much the stock market could change in a day before it was shut down, and we designed a shock absorber (the Federal Reserve Board). That was a century ago. The problem we face today needs a like-minded approach. Namely, political parties of the world will slowly be made irrelevant, unless international monopolistic size restrictions are created. My suggestion for the political parties of the world is to impose the next great limit to the free market system by putting a ceiling on the total level of business (revenues) of multi-national corporations. Otherwise, these political parties may become irrelevant and betray the public trust. We need limits on the size, not just monopoly, of a corporation. It may be time to provide a new shock absorber, though slowly and gradually. Such actions should never be rushed.

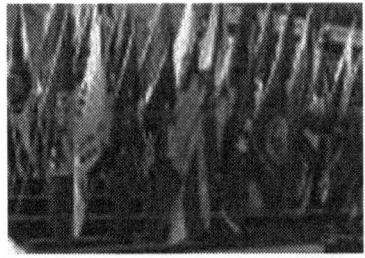

Will flags of businesses replace flags of peoples' nations?

◆　　　◆　　　◆

Consider the following opening comments of a speech delivered by Bill Moyers, November 2001 (and found on the Internet).

This isn't the speech I expected to give today. I intended something else. For the last several years, I've been taking every possible opportunity to talk about the soul of democracy. "Something is deeply wrong with politics today," I told anyone who would listen. And I wasn't referring to the partisan mudslinging, or the negative TV ads, the excessive polling or the empty campaigns. I was talking about something deeper, something troubling at the core of politics. The soul of democ-

racy—the essence of the word itself—is government of, by, and for the people. And the soul of democracy has been dying, drowning in a rising tide of big money contributed by a narrow, unrepresentative elite that has betrayed the faith of citizens in self-government. This wasn't something I came to casually, by the way.

America has gotten so big it has grown away from its people. California's recent People's Initiative that led to the recall of its governor was a welcome point on the scorecard of democracy. Still, that is not to say that democracy is the best for all nations.

America had a great system when the primary tasks of the central government were defense, interstate communication and transportation. However, the tasks the American government have taken on are too numerous. And, having won the Cold War, America has no choice but to step up to the responsibility of maintaining order among nations—a sobering, expensive and serious task. As it is, though, America is staggering under this burden of maintaining order in the new world while dealing with internal over-regulation.

The concept of the *U.S. Constitution* is still good, but I will argue that Thomas Jefferson was right: it is not possible to keep amending the *Constitution* to keep pace with the development of technology. When I was told that Jefferson believed the *Constitution* should be rewritten from scratch every twenty years, it was music to my ears, for I have long maintained that the forefathers should have allowed for a twenty-year-long orderly transitional process for a rewrite of the *Constitution* every 100 years. Individuals go to extreme measures so that the application of law is just and fair, yet few consider the condition of the machine that puts those laws in motion.

◆   ◆   ◆

America is being viewed with fear and adulation by the world. Meanwhile, Americans are rushed and overworked.

If there is Light in the soul,
There will be beauty in the person.
If there is beauty in the person,
There will be harmony in the house.
If there is harmony in the house,
There will be order in the nation.

If there is order in the nation,
There will be peace in the world.

—Chinese Proverb

Is there harmony in the average American home? No! According to this proverb, then, as long as there is no harmony in American homes, we will not see order in the nation or world peace.

"Life is difficult." Those are the first three words of *The Road Less Traveled*, which, mostly by word of mouth, sold over seven million copies in America, a busy nation that does not read much. Why?

Heavily resonating wails about the difficulties of life in these United States comprise the opening two pages of *The 7 Habits of Highly Effective People*, which has not stopped its brisk sales since its publication 15 years ago. Why?

Chicken Soup for the Soul and its subsequent spin-off books have sold 60 million copies. Why are our souls so thirsty? Some of us are suffering from Attention Deficit Disorder, while a lot of us are suffering from a "Spiritual Deficit Disorder."

Mary Eberstadt is a social scientist who wrote *Home Alone America, The Hidden Toll of Day Care, Wonder Drugs and Other Parent Substitutes*. She says,

> *"Of the explosive subjects in America today, none is as cordoned off, as surrounded by rhetorical land mines, as the question of whether and just how much children need their parents—especially their mothers."*

She also maintains that,

> *"Over the past few decades, more and more parents have been spending less and less time at home, and most measures of what social scientists call 'child well-being' have simultaneously been in what once would have been scandalous decline."*

We tell our children to be wary of strangers, but we use TV as an attention manager. What can we do to defend our children's psyches? What do we do to defend our own psyches?

Is globalization only to benefit the powerful and the financiers, speculators, investors and traders! Does it offer nothing to men, women and children who are ravaged by the violence of poverty!

—Nelson Mandela, Leader of the African National Congress
and 1993 Nobel Peace Prize Winner

9

How We Got Here

Today, the major Eastern religions of Buddhism and Hinduism (actually more like philosophies or psychologies) each boasts a billion or more adherents. Among the Abrahamic religions, the Jewish faith has 14 million, the Christian faith has 1.8 billion and the Muslim faith has over 1.3 billion. These major religions guide behavior through faith; therefore, they are most powerful.

This chapter provides a unique perspective on the growth and development of the human race, taking its cue from the Hindu's view of the human psyche.

The central concept of Hindu philosophy is *love*. It has a caste system that is thousands of years old. Since passage of time tends to oversimplify initially profound concepts (just as Islam has been distilled into the simplified criteria of eliminating alcohol and pig meat), the current Hindu caste system is an oversimplification. In its present form, it classifies human beings into four categories:

- The spiritual or religious leader who invokes faith (*Brahman*),

- The warrior or politician who invokes reason (*Kashatree*),

- The businessman, who makes his money work for him (*Benya*), and

- The worker, who works for his money (*Shuder*).

The initial, more profound Hindu philosophy that originated thousands of years ago might have indicated that a human being's psyche is composed of all these four traits at the same time. Different aspects would be manifest in larger degrees, depending on whether a person is in his twenties, thirties, forties, fifties or sixties.

❖   ❖   ❖

This uniquely Hindu concept from India can be merged with the development of Abrahamic faiths to trace and to project the growth and development of humanity as it gradually comes of age.

Let's take a look at pre-civilization man (Pre-*Brahman*) when we were hunter-gatherers. At that time, it took all our energy just to feed ourselves. There was no time for reflective thought about death and the hereafter. Civilizations were formed only when life was organized by humans to conquer time.

The first recorded civilization was in Mesopotamia at the intersection of the Tigris and Euphrates Rivers, a highly fertile area that lent itself to easy agriculture—and what's agriculture but a more efficient hunting and gathering? The remains of an 8,000-year-old civilization, which thrived because of the natural fertility of the five rivers of Ravi, Sutlej, Chenab, Indus and Jhelum, have been discovered in modern day Pakistan. The civilization existed with streets perpendicular to each other, indicating careful city planning. Poor British management through unlined canals has since destroyed the fertility of this area.

Moving on, as the civilizations of the human race created extra time to reflect on life and death, the reflections created the Abrahamic religions in the Middle West, and the Buddhist-Hindu philosophies in the East. The millennia between the dawn of civilization and the Age of Reason represent the *Brahman* phase of the collective human race because the keepers of the hereafter led the way.

❖   ❖   ❖

With the *Brahman* Age came the Age of Faith. Abraham may have provided Noah with the story of Adam and the tree of knowledge. He proposed a phenomenally useful concept: there is only one God. His devotion to that God (100 percent commitment) was demonstrated by the will to sacrifice his son.

Moses was a great organizer and a fan of the number ten. He organized his army with a pyramid scheme; each commander controlled ten people. His concept of the burning bush and the Ten Commandments appealed to the common man. He recognized that numbers were accurate while language was nebulous.

The human spirit, though, is fundamentally born of the heart and not of the head. Over passage of time, any rigid commitment to organization through numbers leads to over-regulation. At the time Jesus was born, society was over-regulated to the extent of dysfunction. He chose the fundamental Hindu tenet of love as his message. I believe that he wanted to dissolve fear through love. Unfortunately, that did not go over very well. St. Paul chose to revise the Old Testament in light of the message of Jesus, which was to do unto others as you would have them do unto you, and wrote the philosophy/theology of Catholicism.

Mohammad was an orphan in a pagan culture in Saudi Arabia. He was exposed to human nature at an early age. He quickly figured out for himself that honesty is the best policy. In his youth he was known for his honesty. He was a shepherd, like most other prophets.

When Mohammad was forty, he went away into solitude. Upon his return, he declared that God had spoken to him through the angel Gabriel. Mohammad was illiterate. The angel Gabriel's first utterance to Mohammad was "Qul," meaning, "read" or "recite" in Arabic.

Islam does not sell God short. The *Qur'an* mixes church and state to address both peace and prosperity. Why go after either prosperity (through security, as the Jews), or peace (through love, as the Christians) if one can ask for both? The daily Muslim prayer repeats 31 times a day a refrain that first asks for peace to be brought upon Mohammad and his descendants as God brought peace upon Abraham and his descendants. It is followed with a refrain that is a prayer for God to bring prosperity for Mohammad and his descendants as he brought prosperity for Abraham and his descendants. There is no need to go for either peace or prosperity. Go for both—peace and prosperity.

The daily prayer also requests that God not allow the followers to go astray from the path of Abraham. In fact, Mohammad picked up the mentality of Abraham. He reinforced the unity of God by emphasizing the equality of man. Islam does not distinguish between a white, black, brown, or yellow person. This is demonstrated annually during Hajj, the annual pilgrimage to Mecca and the birthplace of Abraham. This is why Malcolm X was so affected by this religion.

It should be noted that Islam has two very important hidden assets that are currently lost on the world scene. First, it does not condone a central religious organization that would collect money and operate on that basis. In other words, it discourages organized religion because that leads to corrupt behavior. Second, Islam does not permit interest on money because derivation of financial instruments provides endless possibilities of putting the uninformed at a greater disadvantage than appropriate.

After founding Islam, which seeks both peace *and* prosperity, Mohammad declared himself to be the last in the line of God's prophets. One can only surmise that he did not wish people to go astray again. Mohammad was not exposed to the Hindu system; nor could he have imagined the rise of Islam and the challenge of the Crusades.

Islam flourished for 700 years after the death of Mohammad, which occurred about 1,400 years ago. Around the end of the first millennium, Islamic philosophers recovered and restored the works of the Greeks, and gave them back to the West in the first coordination of civilizations. The threat of Islam led to a violent and emotional response from the Crusaders near the end of the eleventh century.

Ultimately, it was the Mongols (not Christianity or Judaism) that decimated the zenith of Islam. For, as the Mongols gradually started accepting Islam, the new age of reason dawning in the West gradually filled the power vacuum. The new age brought the Western concept of separating church and state, which essentially suggests that the state should govern the affairs of this life. This happens to be related to prosperity, and that the church should confine itself to the afterlife that relates to peace. During Mohammad's time, it was a powerful idea to bring the affairs of state into the proclamations of God, and because of this, Islam grew rapidly. With the dawning of the new age, though, the Abrahamic religions slowly started losing ground to the power of reason. Thus, the human race finally started growing out of the *Brahman* phase into the *Kashatree* phase of its existence.

◆   ◆   ◆

The advent of the Age of Reason in the West can be likened to mankind's shift into the *Kashatree Age.* In the early part of the second millennium, corruption in the Catholic Church grew to a point that Martin Luther caused a reform in Christianity. Protestants are those who are protesting against politics and corruption in the Vatican. Protestant influence grew. The King of England's illegitimate protestant daughter, Elizabeth I, was forced to fight for her life because the Catholic Church had sanctioned her murder. She won the war with the Vatican. That was the beginning of the end of the political power of the Vatican, but influential economics are still there. The Netherlands, on the other hand, is an advanced country where the concept of separation of church and state took root early.

The climate of thought generated by Elizabeth I's victory played the chicken-and-egg scenario with the science of Galileo and Newton, who showed that the heavens (stars) were actually functioning more like a clock rather than mystical, God-driven occult objects. Thus, the Age of Reason strengthened the West over the last three to four hundred years because of mankind's belief in itself, instead of its blind faith in metaphysics.

When the *Qur'an* was written, it was a powerful idea to mix church and state. But times changed with the dawn of the Age of reason, and church took second position to state. This is why the West does well, and my suggestion is that Islam should also separate church and state. Islam is so powerful that it would easily survive such a separation.

One obvious lesson from the above is that Islamic states should start reorganizing along republic-style principles, in order to benefit from what seems to be working today.

◆   ◆   ◆

If we continue with this application of Hindu philosophy, we can see that the next level of development of the collective human consciousness is happening as we live. The *Kashatrees* are gradually giving way to the *Benyas*. The nations of the world are gradually playing second fiddle to the multi-national corporations of the world.

In other words, in the *Benya age*, church as well as state is about to take a back seat to business. The rise of the multi-national corporations in the second half of the 20th century has now gathered so much momentum that the collective economic power of businesses is overtaking the collective economic power of nation-states at the turn of the millennium. The decimation of Iraq, in the interest of multi-national oil firms, may be analogous in this stage of human development as to defeat of the Vatican by Queen Elizabeth I, a few centuries ago.

Take also Microsoft, which is already issuing "passports." The use of the word "passport" indicates that they understand the portals of power are now intellectual, as in the case of businesses; not physical, as in the case of countries. Countries issue passports so that citizens can move across borders in a legitimate fashion. It seems like Microsoft is planning ahead for a world in which only their members will have access to the business cyber-world of Microsoft.

If the transition into this new age is handled with awareness, understanding, empathy and care, it can possibly bring an end to all war. After all, business generally (except the weapons business) does not want to be interrupted by war. This implies that business has a "corporate conscience" and that politicians can control it properly, not compromising current standards of living while bringing equitable prosperity to the world's people to naturally promote peace. It may be overly optimistic to think this can happen.

As a positive and hopeful symbolic act, however, the author has started a new calendar on October 1, 2003, with the hope that the American attack on Iraq (the newest civilization of the *Kashatree* age trying to assist the oldest civilization) will prove to be both a humanistic and prosperous event for the Iraqi people and a positive event for mankind the world over. It remains to be seen.

◆   ◆   ◆

In sum, a millennium ago, the civility of religion (*Brahman*) was sacrificed in the name of God, but the real reason was politics.

For the last three centuries, the civility of politics (*Kashatree*) was given up in the name of patriotism. The real reason used to be economics.

Now, the civility of economics (*Benya*) is under severe tension. Is the civility of economics being abandoned in the name of conservative compassion for peoples' liberation? The real reason could be as old as a territorial dispute.

It appears that the human race is in the process of the next basis for civility: territorial integration. The word of the day for this territorial integration is globalization. Let us hope that the integration will be made civil by developing an international sense of humor.

Globalization is not an option; it is a certainty. The only thing we can control now is the rate of change. It behooves us to slow down the forces of change and manage it, for such rapid change results in bloody emotional synergy.

As we make the transition to the Age of Business, we must keep in mind that this planet is of the people, by the people, for the people. Unless we come to our senses, and keep this worldwide reality in mind, we risk economic as well as political control over us and possibly WWIII.

The political and economic conflicts and complexities of the last few decades have brought before our eyes dangers which even the darkest pessimists of the last century did not dream of.

—Albert Einstein, Mathematician and Physicist

10

Emotional Balance

Currently, mankind is suffering an unprecedented degree of emotional stress.

The August 13, 2003 issue of *USA Today* reported that in Denver, an unusual issue was placed on the ballot. The intent was to "ensure public safety" by "stress-reducing techniques or programs." Now that is an enlightened use of the government's focus.

The proposal, believed to be the first of its kind, does not tell the city how to do it, just to work for it—my kind of approach. According to the report, "The author, Jeff Packman, suggests soothing music in public places, better nutrition in school lunches, meditation, yoga and other steps to ensure municipal tranquility."

Emotional strain within America shows up as addiction to drugs, profane language, and violence. It finds worldwide expression in desperate acts of terrorism. Within America, though, thoughtful wealthy individuals are using money in a constructive way to manage this emotional stress.

For example, billionaire Ted Turner has donated substantial sums of money to the United Nations to bolster its standing effectiveness. The rest of his actions are consistent with his hearty philanthropic attitude towards humanity overall, and not toward a given charity or country, with a hidden agenda. He lost almost a hundred million dollars on "The Goodwill Games." Perhaps some day, the new billionaires of the information economy will do their part. After all, it will take our collective human will to make a significant difference.

One way to get heard

◆   ◆   ◆

We have a great appetite for sensational micro-events, so that we may feed our minds with that which is interesting in the moment. The OJ Simpson trial held America spellbound for a long time. At some level, this spell lasted even longer than that cast by September 11, 2001. It is unfortunate that things that are interesting are many times not important, and things that are important are many times not promoted by the communication media. Celebrity scandals get a lot of attention, for they are promoted as interesting by the media for as long as the public will respond to it.

Thoughtful reflection requires a longer attention span.

A nationally syndicated radio show host was incensed on September 17, 2001 because the FBI had allocated some of its resources to protect Muslim Americans against the backlash of emotions that were understandably running high. He and his callers could not understand why some of the resources were being wasted during such an emergency. The host challenged any Muslim American to call. Before September 11, I was a Pakistani American. September 11 shifted my identity to a Muslim American. So I called.

I argued that the FBI was making intelligent use of its resources. Reducing the fear in the hearts of American Muslims was the best way to uncover any more terrorist cells in the country. No one steps out to cooperate if they feel unsafe. The best place to hide a book is in the library, but the best way to find one is through the librarian. He changed his mind, thanked me for the insight and told me, "Your one phone call made my whole day worthwhile." The generosity of the American individual never ceases to amaze me. And while I have your attention, I think a crash course in Islam would serve everyone well.

◆   ◆   ◆

I am not ashamed to say that I had problems with Islam as a child. As an adult I have come to respect the religion as much as any other. There are many books trying to define Islam. My definition is very simple.

The heart of the religion shows up in the Arabic recitations repeated 31 times a day. They comprise the five mandatory daily prayers performed yoga-style with an attitude of gratitude. The required hygiene promotes health. The yoga-style ritual movements promote body functionality. The Morning Prayer helps you get the day started. Two mid-day prayers interrupt the flow of work. The evening prayer prepares for family time. The bedtime prayer is for sound sleep.

The month of Ramadan takes care of all mental health issues. Everyone understands how a hungry stomach feels. It does not allow room for pointless ruminations. By the time the month is over, the forgotten attitude of gratitude for a full stomach is back in full force.

My current take on Islam is that it is difficult to have physical or mental health problems if you follow the first two of the five prescribed rituals. The five daily prayers take care of the physical and mental, and fasting takes care of the mental also.

Buried in the pages of a 2003 book on Islam are the following, almost reluctant, words: "In the period which European historians see as a dark interlude between the decline of ancient civilization—Greece and Rome—and the rise of modern civilization—Europe—Islam was the leading civilization in the world, marked as such by its great and powerful kingdoms, its rich and varied industry and commerce, its original and creative sciences and letters."

Despite this, we call the heyday of Islam, "The Dark Ages" in our world history books. We must acknowledge the glorious history of Islam that lasted for almost a whole millennium. Violence is caused by lack of acceptance. Fortunately, an understanding of Islam, no matter how rudimentary, is creeping into the Western psyche.

One quarter of the world's population (and growing) is not going to roll over and play dead in a nuclear world. Only the irrationally exuberant suffer from the psychological denial that unjust usurpation of their oil (i.e. the U.S. treaties with Native Americans and Mexico) will be a war worth fighting.

Before September 11, 2001, it was common knowledge that terrorists resort to symbolic action. Immediately after 9/11 the silence about the meaning of 911 (emergency) was understandable. But I can tell you from personal experience that few Muslim Americans understand our nation's long-term silence about the symbolism of 9/11. The current political reality in America is that there are almost as many Muslim Americans now as there are Jewish Americans, and they are friendly with the newly powerful Indian Americans.

Muslim Americans were unwilling to join the countrywide protests before America's historic first pre-emptive strike to disarm another country. Now, there is a deafening silence about the symbolism of 9/11. I happen to know from private conversations that some Muslim Americans deeply regret having voted for George Bush II.

◆   ◆   ◆

A real war is between nations, not between a nation and terrorist groups. Real wars are coming our way. They are caused by misunderstandings and lack of vision, in addition to economic conflict. States as well as businesses are like vehicles with their own momentum. The only difference is that during wars, businesses depend on lawsuits and nations resort to violence, for they have the military at their disposal; and political power shatters economic power.

I have owned and operated many businesses. I have had a few business "accidents," yet in retrospect, the causes were always avoidable; I had just become too comfortable. Eternal vigilance is the price of leadership. If my business is on a collision course with another entity, be it a competitor, a client, a supplier, a bank, an insurance agency or a bonding agency, and I do not rise to the challenge of avoiding the conflict, then the causes of the collision are poor foresight, slow response time, poor maneuverability, distraction, or a failed system.

Three months after September 11, the Christmas break came and muffled the "wakeup call" in its celebrative spirit. The world's politicians and economists went back to business as usual; they know no other way.

I agree that we must not negotiate with terrorists. Yet it is necessary to create and convey a worldwide vision of a just method of governing, which may be twenty or so years in the making. In these stressful times, we all need hope in order to be pacified.

Language emanates from the heart and engineering from the brain.

—Dr. Joe Jacobs, from *The Compassionate Conservative*

11

Varying Realities

Language is the second closest bond after blood, thus it is of primary importance in the exchange of ideas, creation of worldviews and interaction of cultures. England may have lost the war when America declared independence, but it retained considerable influence through the bond of language.

One third of the world's books are published in English. English is the language of two back-to-back world dominant civilizations. Official business in India, Pakistan and Bangladesh is still conducted in English. The most popular subject in school in China is English. Add in Australia, Canada, South Africa, New Zealand, to name just a few, and it becomes clear that English is the language of the world.

In longitudes east of England, the word "spin" is used for the spinning motion of a ball in play. In America, the word "spin" holds an additional meaning; it describes the intentional weaving of words to promote a certain agenda. And in America, the word "English" also holds an additional meaning; it is often used instead of the word "spin" to describe the spinning motion of a ball in play. The prodigal son is still cautious of the domineering mother.

Remember, language and thought are interdependent and have a connection with the group's perception of reality. China, for instance, lives in a different reality than the rest of the world.

The different Chinese reality is caused by the different construct of their languages, which use symbols instead of an alphabet of letters to construct words and various combinations of words. Their concepts of the words Wu and Li have been celebrated by Gary Zukav, for they correctly describe the many different ways that one can perceive our world. We need to open our eyes to different realities for, they, too, play roles on the world stage.

In *The Wealth of Nations*, Adam Smith noted that China, in terms of its commerce, does not move forward or backward. Nonetheless, the most recent Chinese reality has shifted. China has declared its own birthday to be on October 1, the first day of the fiscal year of the American federal government. This new commitment to become America's trading partner has borne fruit. Economic power quickly translates to political and military power. China's power in the 21st century should not be underestimated. By savvy number management, China is on a fast track of expansion.

◆　　　◆　　　◆

Some think that life is best managed by numbers, and to a great extent they are right, but research at The Johnson O'Connor Foundation's human engineering laboratory indicates that success in life is relatable to only one factor: [English] vocabulary.

Word-oriented people are probably right brain dominated, and so navigate through life focusing on people instead of time and money. Should they also learn the mental discipline of reading and writing, they can actually use language to transcend time. Aristotle and Shakespeare are good examples of such people. Should these same people learn the discipline of love, they can grace us with theocracies, monarchies, and aristocracies.

Deepak Chopra, an M.D., suggests that he is a prisoner of his own words. Dr. Joseph Jacobs, an engineer, is fascinated with the tyranny of words. Tom Friedman, a journalist, calls his book about the post-September 11 situation a word album. He sees words as a means of illustration. Elliot Aronson, a social psychologist, thinks of himself as a word factory. I would like to think of myself as a person who liberates our minds of the unintended tyranny caused by misunderstood words.

I have one suggestion for America: add "Muslim" when you talk about the Judeo-Christian faiths. "Much of the rest of the world is already using the term, "Jewish/Christian/Muslim." Or, use the word "Abrahamic" as an umbrella term when referring to the three faiths. Such language naturally conveys acceptance. Acceptance goes a long way towards creating good feelings.

Everyone agrees that spoken language can be vague. Yet few eschew obfuscation☺. Some of us actually take time to fuss over the inappropriate connotations assigned to words that are placed out of context.

Then there is the language of numbers. Mathematics communicates in numbers; it is the only precise and reliable language. Engineers are the mainstream product of applied physics and mathematics, both exact sciences.

My guess is that numbers-oriented people are left-brain dominant, and thus get stuck in the quantifiable worlds of time and money. Accounting is a game of numbers that creates a highly manipulative reality. Cash basis, versus accrual, versus completed contract, is the beginning. Creative accounting becomes finance. The word "mental," in such cases, could be an adjective for the effort needed to cope with both time and money.

Despite this, or maybe, for this reason, numbers best sustain organizational structure, which in turn tends to produce prosperity. Numbers live in a sea of rules (law). It is the legal system that validates numbers; however, it checks up on itself so much that it chokes itself.

◆   ◆   ◆

Games observe rules as do numbers. Because of this, many have come to realize that one of the best ways to live life is to view and play it as a game to the extent possible. Games, such as chess, use a level playing field with boundaries that are in plain view. That provides the players, referees, and spectators real-time feedback. They start with a setup (starting positions of pieces on the board) and an objective (capture the king). The rules are clear about what is allowed (how each piece may move) and what is not allowed (restrictions on the ways pieces may move). In other words, barriers and freedoms are clearly defined.

In today's "globalized" world, many problems are created because the "game conditions" differ, and the playing field is not as level or as well defined as it is in chess, or even in a video game. Mastering the use of words and numbers is sometimes not enough to play the game well.

The first goal of the game of life is, and always will be, to survive. The secondary goals of human life are to ensure long-term survival and strengthen control over one's environment. In the *Brahman* age, the ultimate goal of life was to please God. In the *Kashatree* age, it shifted to the accumulation of power through politics. In the *Benya* age, it is shifting to the accumulation of power through money.

A stitch in time saves nine.

—British Proverb

12

Is WWIII the Synthesis?

Niall Ferguson, one of the most prominent historians of our time, has written a series of books documenting the history of power in the last three centuries. In his 2001 book, *The Cash Nexus*, he states that WWI and WWII could have been avoided. His 2003 book, *Empire: The Rise and Demise of the British World Order and the Lessons for Global Power*, moves on to alert us to the lessons America can learn from England's history of global power.

Even he misses the point that we should be proactively and purposefully working on avoiding WWIII. Eric Lee of Toronto wrote a strong rebuttal in which he reminded Ferguson that his dreams of an English-dominated empire are too early, for China will not forget what England did to that country by pushing opium on the whole nation. If China and the West are continuing to underestimate each other's power, even at such highly intellectual levels, both sides will naturally perceive the other as cavalier at best, and arrogant at worst. Such situations lead to tensions. Then some small, unforeseen events cause quick realignments of alliances and positions. Such times of political turmoil have resulted in World Wars.

◆   ◆   ◆

The great German philosopher, Georg Hegel, believed that humanity progresses in cycles. Basically, there is a thesis, or state of affairs. Every state of affairs, however, bears within it internal conflicts, the seeds of its own destruction. With passage of time, an antithesis (alternative to state of affairs) develops. Once the antithesis gathers enough momentum, there is a clash between the thesis and the antithesis, and a synthesis emerges. We can apply this way of thinking to anticipate the direction of the world's current affairs. Who knows, maybe the Hegelian Absolute (the ultimate and final synthesis) is really a Golden Era of Peace.

Hegel

I see the last great thesis as being the American *Constitution*. It created political stability and a decent balance between the power of government and the individual. In the cradle of stability, the nation became strong enough to resolve the conflict between the nations of the second world twice in the last century, in two World Wars.

An antithesis, however, has been gaining sufficient political momentum through improvements in technologies of communication and transportation, which, as I've argued, have made bedfellows of the East and West.

Unless we are careful, WWIII may be the impending synthesis. It can start in an unforeseen area of the third world and produce the domino effect that precipitated WWI and WWII. This impending synthesis, namely the East-West confrontation, is inevitable and, without proper management, will undoubtedly be the most dangerous such synthesis in history because it will involve a much broader, worldwide concentration of forces, and probably force the politicians to use nuclear weapons.

The current emphasis on "fighting terrorism" is like taking our eyes off the road to swat a fly on the car window while a truck is headed straight for the car. It is up to us to make this coming synthesis intellectual through unusually tolerant diplomacy.

Gross national happiness is more important than gross national product.

—Bhutanese King Jigme Singye Wangchuk

13

Psychology of Nations

In psychology, a cognitive distortion is the alteration that our psyche assigns to our worldview. It is the lens through which we view the world. Some cognitive distortions are common to all people. One such cognitive distortion is called psychological projection. It is best described as our habit of assuming that others think and feel as we do. Nations are prone to psychological projection as are individuals.

During a drive from Los Angeles to Las Vegas, I stopped at a gas station. I went inside the kiosk to pay for the gasoline I was about to purchase. The lady at the cash register was disconcerted. Uninvited, she confided in me that the last person had left without paying for the gasoline. She went on a diatribe that lasted for about five minutes, during which time she told me that she and her husband were so honest that they reported even their cash income on their tax returns.

And then, "How can this man do this to people like us?" She was doing what most of us do. We expect others to treat us like we treat them. But that expectation is only sustainable if we think that others believe as we believe, have the same goals as we do, use the same thought process that we use, and so on. That is a broad and often inaccurate assumption.

Birds of the same feather flock together because they have some commonality in their psyches. This is why first-generation Americans understand each other, and are even closer if they are of the same ethnicity. Such natural segregation among humans creates inertia, and makes it difficult to change the ways of the community, even if the changes are for the better.

One of the major problems we are now facing is that nations of the world are all busy projecting their own psychologies on others.

The way to give hope to the people of the world is through balanced discipline and a wider worldview.

◆   ◆   ◆

Sir Winston Churchill was wise to Hitler long before anyone else. During his tenure as Great Britain's prime minister, he drank heavily. I believe that was his defense mechanism. My guess is, he would have been immobilized by the gravity of the situation England faced without the temporary relief provided by alcohol. It is hard to maintain serenity, when you see two trains heading toward each other on a collision course, while you watch helplessly. Each minute becomes an hour. For such problems, we all need psychological defense mechanisms.

The dictionary defines a psychological defense mechanism as: "Any of various, usually unconscious, mental processes, including denial, projection, rationalization, and repression, that protect the ego from shame, anxiety, conflict, loss of self-esteem, or other unacceptable feelings or thoughts."

> ***Psychological denial****: An unconscious defense mechanism characterized by refusal to acknowledge painful realities, thoughts or feelings.*

> ***Psychological projection****: The attribution of one's own attitudes, feelings, or suppositions to others: "Even trained anthropologists have been guilty of unconscious projection of clothing the subjects of their research in theories brought with them into the field." (Alex Shoumatoff)*

> ***Rationalization:*** *A defense mechanism by which your true motivation is concealed by explaining your actions and feelings in a way that is not threatening.*

> ***Psychological repression****: The unconscious exclusion of painful impulses, desires, or fears from the conscious mind.*

> ***Ego****: The self, especially as distinct from the world and other selves. In psychoanalysis, the division of the psyche that is conscious, most immediately controls thought and behavior, and is most in touch with **external reality**.*

Individuals live in varying depths of *external reality*. Those, who follow the path of least resistance, live with less risk; therefore, they need fewer defense mechanisms. This is probably why Aristotle suggested the virtue of the mean value; Buddha taught the middle way; and Mohammad said, "All average things are good." But I doubt that they followed the middle way themselves. We are, after all, who we are.

People navigate their lives using a variety of psychological defense mechanisms. My mother-in-law goes for the moral high ground. My sister-in-law resorts to silence. My second oldest sister gets angry. My oldest brother uses religion. My niece uses humor. God bless her soul. She and her friend Norma have gone back from sunny California to live in dreary England. The reason: "Nobody thinks in the US."

Thought is my default defense mechanism. When faced with a challenge to my ego (or even to the ego of another; unless I am pulling a prank), I try to gain perspective though *the study of* and *reflection upon* the *broader situation* within which the problem has arisen.

So my natural inclination is to deepen my level of understanding to a point where I can see all sides of the problem. Another way to say this is that I start mentally examining a larger map of reality. More often than not, I succeed in my pursuit of a broader map of reality.

For example, I had much trouble buying into the concept of "turning the other cheek," until I learned that, in the original language of Aramaic, this phrase means, "taking a fresh look." The idea is to reposition the angle of one's face to see if a different view would shed light on the perplexing matter of inappropriate behavior by others.

Larger maps of reality often permit creative solutions that produce "win all" results. Because, like most engineers, I am careful, I conduct small-scale experiments to see whether my broader map works. Once I am satisfied that my mental map of reality works, I try and help others understand it so they can benefit from my realizations. This has sometimes been a mistake, for not everyone is interested in or has the attention span for the broader map that I have created in my mind. The typical response is that I think too much. For this, my defensive retort is, "You don't think enough, for thinking is the hardest work there is."

◆   ◆   ◆

I have not changed my mind about nuclear non-proliferation since I was fifteen. It is a pipe dream, and yet our nations need a defense mechanism to be able to function. The only half-hope, away from nuclear proliferation, is the United Nations, which never functioned well. Who will keep the winds of change that are now sweeping across the planet from creating a new reign of terror akin to the 1792 reign of terror in France, in which the common man started killing the aristocrat next door?

The track record lawyer-politicians have in avoiding war offers little comfort. As noted earlier, all schools of political economics still preach that wars between nations are caused by economic conflict. Avoiding the coming synthesis between the East and the West requires vision, not a fixation on the gross national product.

By hoping that non-proliferation will work, we are living in [fearful] psychological denial. If one accepts the proliferation of nuclear weapons as inevitable, it is easier to focus on containment. For example, if a nation announces a test detonation, there could be an international agreement that its threatened neighbors have a cooling off period of six months. Such a thought pattern would have avoided the knee jerk reaction by Pakistan to detonate immediately after India, thereby avoiding an extremely unstable situation.

There is a saying from the Indian subcontinent: "Hope creates stability." The terrorists of the world lost faith in the system of governments and, therefore, have no hope that any actions other than terror can make their lives better, or bring justice as they see it. Like I've said elsewhere, if there is genuine hope, people can be patient.

...not to believe in the possibility of dramatic change is to forget that things have changed, not enough, of course, but enough to show what is possible. We have been surprised before in history. We can be surprised again. Indeed, we can do the surprising.

—Howard Zinn, Author of *A People's History of the United States* covering the period 1945–1960

14

Change

Our resistance to change is caused by fear and inertia. Fear of the unknown can be useful, but it has a tendency to apply defensive strategies at inappropriate times. For example, a fearfully loud noise may cause a muscle reaction while driving a car, which may cause one to swerve and crash. The inertia of doing or believing something different is based in what we are used to, lazily hanging on to our old ways, and being skeptical about new information that may lead us in a different direction, to a different conclusion.

Our subconscious and unconscious minds are slower to adapt to change than our conscious one. As we grow older, for example, we add fat to our bodies. This could be a carryover from centuries ago, when we had to store excess food energy as we grew older for fear we would not be able to get it otherwise. The body has not adapted to the fact that our society no longer has a need for this.

John Gray's book, *Men Are from Mars, Women Are from Venus,* states that men get their sense of self from their achievements and women from the quality of their relationships. Yet it fails to mention that we humans get our sense of self from being right. That is called vesting. If we have vested our whole lives in believing a certain view, we get shaken to the core if different realities hit us.

Even though the National Aeronautics and Space Administration (NASA) has landed people or rockets 50 times on the moon, and they can easily give us the schedule for the month of Ramadan for the next 100 years, the Muslims of the world still look up to the sky and squabble over the starting date of Ramadan, depending on the sighting of the moon.

The collective consciousness is also slow to learn and adapt. We hear so many new opinions and ideas that it is hard to tell which ones will withstand the test of time. So we reserve our credence until we gather more evidence. It takes us enormous amounts of time to accept newer, proven realities. Galileo robbed the Vatican of its authenticity and Queen Elizabeth I robbed the Vatican of its power hundreds of years ago, yet we continue paying our religious dues.

Somehow, we feel a sense of personal failure when our lifelong views are challenged. When the challenge is too much to comprehend, we tend to rescind, falling prey to righteousness for our original views.

Collective righteousness leads to wars among nations. Similar to the management of technology being at the heart of most industrial progress, the management of collective thought and nations' views of each other just might be at the heart of the progress of peace.

◆   ◆   ◆

Change manifests in many different ways. September 11 provided occasions for several case studies. In the case of media reporting, I saw profit-driven absurdities rise, especially with respect to terrorism. In the words of Jay Leno,

> *"It's like the networks are a how-to manual for terrorists. You see them on the news. The reporter is standing outside a water treatment plant going, 'If they poured the poison here, it could wipe out thousands because the guard is off duty from noon until one every day.'"*

On a similar note, in late summer of 2003, my favorite TV show, *60 Minutes*, aired a segment saying that Canada is a perfect staging ground for terrorists to attack America. They argued that the 5,500 mile-long border is quite porous and that the Canadian law that governs immigration is quite lax. They actually *stated* the words one might say in order to be let go free in Canada! I was astonished.

◆   ◆   ◆

Humanity's ego has suffered a few major blows over the course of history. First, the realization that mother Earth is not the center of the universe must have made some people wonder why the God of Christianity chose to make man in his own image. Second, the realization that the Vatican has neither legitimacy (Galileo, who was officially pardoned in the late 20th century) nor power (Elizabeth I, whose descendants have still not been smitten by God) has been treated with much *psychological denial*. Third, the thought that we are just another species of life brought so much grief to our ego that even the law upheld our psychological denial, as it returned a guilty verdict against the man who chose to teach Darwin in the Skokie trial of the State of Tennessee.

The astute must have realized then that the baton of providing psychological comfort was being officially passed on from the church to the state. Therefore, nations must take the lead in managing the transfer of change to effect world peace while they still have the opportunity.

Prior to the French reign of terror that started in 1792, it is doubtful that the French aristocrats saw what was coming. The world is a much larger place than France. It would be wise for the aristocrats of today's world to be careful, lest their ivory towers come crashing down among slogans of, "God is great."

But first things first. Change is constant, and possibilities are endless. The species that balances its rate of internal change to the rate of external change will survive. There is a reasonable likelihood that the inability of the human race to adapt to its external reality will bring our story to an abrupt end. Those who wish to ignore this possibility are doing so at their own peril and the peril of their fellow inhabitants of earth.

When I first wrote down my thoughts in 1994, the whole notion of World War III was far from everyone's mind. We were happy about the recently won Cold War, and the dawning of the Internet. I have regretted not publishing my 1994 manuscript. Publishing this one is my way of fulfilling my duty to the human race.

I know that my unity with all people cannot be destroyed by national boundaries and government orders.

—Leo Tolstoy, Russian Novelist

15

My Message

There are compelling arguments that the human race is not paying attention to a huge conflict that will likely occur in a few decades between the East and the West. My purpose is to launch a message of world peace, which I will endeavor to sustain for the remainder of my life.

The side benefit to you as an individual is that you will gain many insights that will assist you in your personal life. Regardless of whether you choose to believe what is said here, this global perspective will assist you in navigating correctly through the rapidly evolving world in which we live.

As I have said, in his book, *The Cash Nexus*, Niall Ferguson argues that WWI and WWII could have been avoided. His focus was on history. His next book should have said WWIII can be avoided. I am an engineer and a businessman. Therefore, my focus is on the future. I am picking up where Ferguson left off. I am also picking up the peace proclamation from Ted Turner quoted in the book, *NLP: The New Technology of Achievement* (1994), as saying,

> *We have to take responsibility...to have influence in our communities. And our community...is not just the local market or even our country, but the world in which we live.*

> *Why don't we aim, during the next ten years to have peace on earth? And in the year 2000, turn the time back to Zero? And let it be B.P. and A.P.—Before Peace and After Peace. That could be the greatest honor we could bestow upon our generation. So if we do that, then people will be here two thousand years from now...*

◆　　◆　　◆

The last time I went to the other side of the world was six years ago. Just as Americans confuse Iran to be an Arabic nation or Pakistan to be part of the Middle East, the citizens of these countries confuse England with America. All the

Middle Easterners see is oil in Muslim lands under Western control. After the attack on Iraq, my bet is that they feel America is now adopting the Israeli policy of "pre-emptive strikes." Actually, everyone is becoming paranoid. My message to the world is, "relax!" and "pay attention" to "the right stuff."

As the world is distracted by the war on terrorism, we should pay attention to the proliferation of nuclear weapons and the way nations are treating each other. This is accompanied by rapid momentum in the East. After WWII, we helped Japan become the second largest economy. Now, China and India are coming on strong.

Now is the time to get oriented about the Orient and help the Orient get oriented about the Occident. This is a huge task that will take many, many years and must be started now. The shadow of nuclear weaponry is both a crisis and an opportunity. It is an opportunity for humanity to bring an end to all war as well as bring sanity to this planet.

Some scholars describe the history of man as a chronology of wars interrupted only by two major historical non-violent events; the birth of Jesus and the invention of the printing press. The Internet is here. We can communicate with people all over the world in real time; and communication is one of the keys to understanding. The press and the Internet are some of the few solutions available for independent, coordinated communication. We should use them heavily and effectively.

◆   ◆   ◆

Albert Einstein had a few sayings that are pertinent.

"Common sense is the collection of prejudices we acquire by age eighteen."

I agree. Yet we can attempt to shed our preconceived notions.

"The significant problems of the day cannot be solved at the level of thinking that created them."

The question is: how can we expand our thinking to grasp the big picture, and thus work to solve our problems from a global perspective?

Some men see things as they are and say, "Why?" I dream of things that never were and say," Why not?"

—George Bernard Shaw, Irish Playwright and Social Spokesman

16

My Stand

I feel much kinship with the Founding Fathers of America because they understood business and proclaimed independence from England, invoking the Laws of Nature and Nature's God.

Emerson and Thoreau connect with me through their essays. Although I am not from Massachusetts, I attended Harvard, as they did. In the course of my life's events I have gained profound insights which changed me on the inside while the container (body) in which I live looks the same. This causes much misunderstanding. Emerson talks about this kind of thing.

What transpired within me is this. I gave up the blind pursuit of money in 1989 and focused on understanding women. Twice since then, I have undergone profound internal change. First, in April 1991, at age 43, I went to an ontology workshop in Orange County, California. People asked me what happened during those five days. I responded, "I was born again." "Can you explain better?" they pressed on. I said, "I had a five-day life experience." That seemed to satisfy most people. And yet, my walk and talk have been much different since then.

Second, during the summer of 2003, on June 15, I had a mystical experience encompassing about forty insights, and the book in your hand was written then. I stopped updating it on September 3, 2003.

Shortly thereafter, I chose to struggle out of the time and money trap without the help of my family and nominated Naf, a young woman who understood me and had recently graduated from the University of California at Berkley as a Dean's List Philosophy major, as the keeper of my trust. That same day I made two female strangers and my sister laugh for about an hour each. I think it was the most successful day of my life.

The author believes that Nature's God does not want us to impress him with our words; he wants us to impress him with our actions. Therefore, on September 24, 2003, I started an organization, intended to be a political party, for the use of humanity. For this purpose, I recorded the name, "My Use International" as a business entity. I am now in the business of life, and in the business of peace. I have graduated from America's school of, "We are in the business of business."

I am spending my own hard-earned "after tax" dollars to breathe life into this vehicle (www.myuse.org) from which I will withdraw as soon as practical. One of its objectives is to provide a forum for worldwide, uncensored dialogue on the subject of world peace and an end to war.

Perhaps it should be noted here that the similarity between the sound of "My Use" and the Indian term for "utter disappointment in the half-witted actions of mankind" ("*mayoos*") is no accident. My heart belongs to India because of that nation's commitment to love and non-violence.

The next nation that declares war will be held accountable by humanity, the keepers of My Use International.

A journey of a thousand miles begins with a single step.

—Confucius

17

Step One: Preparation for Change

This chapter is devoted to discussing a few concepts towards orienting the East and West to one another. This is essential if a coming synthesis is to be constructive, and not destructive.

Naming the reconstructed structure at ground zero "World Peace Center" would be a symbolic start. There are influential people in the world, leaders who have retired. They, too, should have signs outside their places reading, "World Peace Center." I have visited with at least one (former Pakistan Foreign Minister Agha Shahi) and communicated with another (Mikhail Gorbachev). It is all just a matter of gaining critical momentum.

More importantly, we all need to be educated and informed. Those who have studied the problems facing the world in the 21st century are calling attention to morality and ethics as the central problem, rather than to the standard concerns about nuclear warfare (expressed here) and other global threats. We need to pay attention to them.

On the one hand, we denigrate conformity as "political correctness" and not as ethical and moral conversation and action. On the other hand, we cry out for a sense of conscience and morality. What a bunch of hypocrites we have become.

Dedicating a whole section of the reconstructed New York World Trade Center to educating the world on the subject of vanishing morality in the face of capitalist advances would be a good investment. This vanishing morality is neither good nor bad, only thinking makes it so. America and the West are confronting a difficulty in this area. What they need is help from the East, not judgmental behavior.

We are coming into times when the world will need to tolerate and accept, even without total understanding. Otherwise, we risk digging our own graves.

◆   ◆   ◆

There is a joke that illustrates the condition of order in third world countries whose resources are not sufficient for proper management. It dates backs to the days of the Soviet Union. It goes like this:

> The Soviets are officially atheists, yet when they come to Pakistan, they start believing in God. Why?…"***Someone*** must be running this place!"

Another joke is commonly known among many third world countries. I heard it in Pakistan, while I was growing up there. It goes like this:

> "I have come up with a brilliant idea on how to manage our nation…. Let us attack America, and when we lose the war, they will end up making our country the 51st state."

The point here is that everyone looks up to the United States. Therefore, America is in a unique position to lead and provide a vision of an intellectual synthesis. A clear vision of a just world will go a long way towards strengthening the moderates against the fundamentalists in the East.

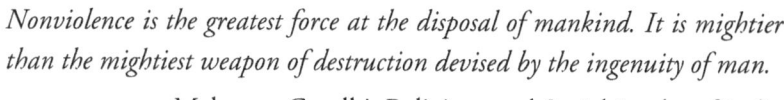

Nonviolence is the greatest force at the disposal of mankind. It is mightier than the mightiest weapon of destruction devised by the ingenuity of man.

—Mahatma Gandhi, Religious and Social Leader of India

18

Step Two: Managing Change

Orientation is the first step towards a peaceful co-existence. Just as important, and urgent, is the management of global change. There are various ways to do this. For example, My Use International is now a political party registered in California for the use of humanity. Its first order of business is to send another wake-up call to America, using California as its physical base.

My Use International is my commitment to a sustained effort towards peace for the people of the world. It can be tapped whenever humanity is ready.

◆   ◆   ◆

Catalysts of change can be gradually implemented with built-in mechanisms, such as televised open forums and real-time Internet opinion polls, to cope with the political resistance that naturally builds against all types of change (even if the resistance is for the positive). Books and discussions about them are generally effective in slowly bringing about such change.

Whatever we do must be done slowly and with full disclosure. Obtaining consensus across nations that have "not walked in the other's shoes" is where the difficulty lies. In addition, we must remember the lessons of history. That, everyone will agree upon.

Protests can bring about positive change. The motives of protesters are usually pure, and their intent is remarkably altruistic. Protests fall into two categories. The first is the last minute, one-time protest against an impending event. The last minute protests against the impending war on Iraq are a good example of such work. They were not too little, but they were too late. The military was already deployed and in position. The cost of not attacking could have been even higher by that time. Few have the foresight—or foreknowledge—to proactively plan such protests.

The second category of protest, civil disobedience, is more effective. The process of civil disobedience is a sustained effort against an unhealthy and unjust trend. It does not end with the completion of an act. Such sustained resistance takes its toll, and brings about peaceful change in a managed way. But the activity must be sustained and well organized to avoid disastrous results, such as the blood bath that occurred in 1947 during the partition of India and Pakistan. America is ripe for such a movement to be led by the baby boomers in this decade. And with the help of the engineering community, I believe orchestrating such an effort with result is possible.

Engineering is one of the few professions that has the mental model suitable for today's situation. Engineers can easily craft a grand vision of the future democracy of the world. I feel that the people of the world would be well served if engineers worked on developing social skills and repositioning themselves as "thoughtful members of a society suffering from ADD (Attention Deficit Disorder)." Thought—not emotion—is needed by our world now.

Words of love may produce loving worlds, but they wisp away. Only words of love *and* work, tempered by numbers of reason and the reputation of the engineering profession, may create a lasting world of worth.

It is true that generally engineers do not go to protest rallies. The engineer's approach is to understand the problem and then design a solution. Engineers are patient. Engineers, I beseech you, be proactive and begin working on the solutions together. Participate in your community's formally structured social environment. Run for congressional and senatorial seats. You may surprise yourselves.

It is okay to make mistakes and take an intellectual risk. To motivate you beyond your intellectual resistance, I refer to author Elbert Hubbard's quote, "Constant effort and frequent mistakes are the stepping stones to genius." Remember, even the three great Greek philosophers (Socrates, Plato, and Aristotle) made major mistakes.

One idea would be to create an Internet discussion group called World Engineering and send in good ideas to your political party. Or start your own independent group. Act, don't just try. And do not worry about looking bad or hurting some individuals' feelings. The task is too urgent and important to worry about social niceties.

Let the existing political parties come up with the particulars of world cooperation that works. After all, they are the ones under threat of losing power to the businesses of the world.

◆   ◆   ◆

Political will lies in the hands of the political parties and the governing regimes of the nations of the world. The *U.S. Constitution* was written in the wake of a war for independence. It intelligently filled a necessary void of power. It was wise to scrap the *Articles of Confederation*, which gave no military to the federal government, thus making it irrelevant. The Founding Fathers corrected their mistake through a complete rewrite. The difference when thinking about a governed world is that while the U.S. military protects the United States as a whole, the world as a whole does not need protection from other worlds. So, a governed world need not have strength by a world military when other means such as trade, public and political opposition, and reason vis-à-vis a world constitution could discipline a rogue nation without destruction and expense.

The Founding Fathers strengthened the central government too much, however, so they came right back with ten amendments, the Bill of Rights. One can see their vacillation in events of history. Thoughtful people do not mind looking bad by vacillating on important decisions. This is what differentiated Jimmy Carter from the other U.S. presidents of my lifetime. Make changes where and when changes are needed.

An issue that the American nation faced in the late eighteenth century was "freedom of speech." An issue we are facing now, with the advent of streaming video and TV networks being owned by a handful of corporations, is "freedom of thought." I am glad that the thin veneer of credibility surrounding TV news is coming off, as the public realizes they must believe in sources that are more credible. It is understandable why there is so much media-bashing these days. Tony Schwartz named his book, *Media, the Second God.* And why was Bernard Goldberg's 2003 book, *Bias: A CBS Insider Exposes How the Media Distort the News,* such a hit? Sure, TV is more powerful than radio and newspapers, but the public is savvy. Most of us know that many news items are actually thinly disguised commercials. Teaser lines for stories on "News at 11" have become an art form.

If the television news media were to take themselves lightly, things would be better. It is the overly deep commitment to look proper that gives the appearance of impropriety. Until then, as I stated earlier, the press and the Internet seem to be two of the few solutions still available for independent, coordinated communication, which is exactly what everyone needs.

Despite this, new laws that address the Bill of Rights in a TV world, and the bill of promises in a "politics for sale" world, must be enacted. Things of this nature can only be done by slow change and a rewrite of the very document that brought the U.S. into existence. To extend this thinking further, should we be working on a Constitutional rewrite, or on something far greater, such as a World Constitution with safeguards against power abuse? That is the question—no longer is it, "To be, or not to be."

The political will to do this for the good of all exists among thoughtful, solution-oriented people. Do such people occupy the majority of the Congress? I think not. What will it take for the other people of the world to see this need, and to assert the will to create a harmonious coexistence?

◆   ◆   ◆

Thus far, these words of mine are just cries in the wilderness. After reading this, will you go back to life as usual? Or will you vow to live congruently with your higher self, which happens to be the same as the health of the small planet we inhabit?

PART III

PROCLAMATION

Messages to the 21st Century from the perspective of Nature's God

…We recognize that there are many problems in our society which are a source of conflict and violence…We dedicate ourselves to working with our neighbors, near and far, day in and day out, to build that peaceful society in which the tragedies we have known are a bad memory and a continuing warning.

—Betty Williams, Northern Irish Peace Activist
and 1976 Nobel Peace Prize Winner

19

To People

WAKE UP TO NATURE! PAY ATTENTION TO THAT WHICH MATTERS MOST AND HAVE FAITH IN ME!

There is one God.
—Abraham

All men are equal.
—Mohammad

There is one soul. It is related to the world.
—Ralph Waldo Emerson

All People

When in the course of human events, some of you declared independence in 1776, you invoked the Laws of Nature and My Laws (The Laws of **Nature's God**), to show respect for the views and opinions of the rest of humanity. Those courageous souls among you did not invoke *Abraham's God* or *Buddha's God*, and yet, I bestowed upon them and their descendants what Mohammad (and his followers) requests of God (Allah) incessantly in the five yoga-style prayers each day.

Why is the Muslim religion, Islam, which is the youngest of the four billion-member faiths, expanding at the fastest rate? Listen to Nature's God.

You have all made mistakes. You will all make many more mistakes. So do not rush to judgment. Be not the first to cast a stone. Accept your mistakes, forgive yourselves—and say, "Now what?"—and move on. Accept your past, but live in accordance with your vision of the future.

Believe geography, for it can be checked; and physics, for it can be proven. But treat politics, philosophy and psychology with a healthy dose of skepticism.

Beware of languages and civilizations. Their cradles give birth to great comforts, but they are not beyond question. Stop the lunacy. Learn to get along with each other and live together in peace on My wonderful Earth.

Relax! Follow My course! I will help those who help themselves and others.

Have faith in Me, in yourselves, and in humanity. Once the stomach is fed, and you are safe, relax about the rest.

Beware of unbridled civilization! At the end of the hunter-gatherer stage, you stored food, which gave you time to think; you used language to create political bonds. To live this life, you must pass judgment, and yet, your judgment is the seed of your destruction, so do not get too attached to your views. Be open to updating your maps of reality, your worldviews. Absolutism will kill you.

Newton proved there is no absolute rest in space. Einstein showed there is no absolute time in life. All knowledge is relative. Understand that there are no absolute truths in your lives. *Everything is relative.* Have faith in the elders among you who are peaceful and prosperous.

You and your communities will never understand each other completely, but you can respect each other. Reserve all praise for Nature's God, and be respectful to yourself and others—all others.

Lasting peace comes from mutual respect. Lasting prosperity comes from faith and organization. Your way to salvation is to have faith in one God (Nature's God). Believe in the equality of man, respect your elders, and have faith in all men, communities, businesses, nations and organizations. Believers will be rewarded with security, peace, love, acceptance, serenity and harmony.

Jews

Publicize the fact that you are living in the year 5,764 after the death of Abraham, while the rest of the world is living in the third millennium. Naturally, you think of yourselves as the chosen ones, if only by virtue of your endurance.

The Laws of Moses are the laws of mankind.

Some among you say, "All I am required to do is 'Understand myself, understand others, and be humble.'" You will never understand others completely. Therefore, your knowledge will make you ignorant to some and arrogant to others, and your humility will be lost in the ripple effect of your past choices. Pay attention to Shakespeare's message from *The Merchant of Venice*. Is a pound of flesh worth so much blood?

Security and safety does not come from money; it comes from the way you have treated others.

It is better to be kind than to be right.

In your salvation lies the salvation of the human race, so *redirect your attention and don't build walls.*

Muslims

Relax! You are devout followers of your faith, and yet your plight should tell you what Nature's God thinks of your mindlessness. Only I may judge, and even I am choosing to wait until judgment day! Step up to the plate of competition in accordance with the non-violent Laws of Nature.

Leadership has its burdens. You are reaping the benefits of the West's technological advances. Be grateful.

Elders

Money and time are traps for your lives. To escape them, nominate young people you trust, to be the keepers of your lives. This will give you mental clarity and comfort. This way you will become the denominators of the human race. The human race needs you for its stability. You are the last great hope of humanity.

Get out of the business of business before you are too old to get into the business of life. Nominate your children and your descendants as the keepers of your trust. Do not put your trust in money; put your money in trustworthy hands.

Understand your children. Do not make them as you are. They are the ones who also truly understand you and may have the courage to give you advice that is tailored to your life.

Wake up from your indifference, as did the West in the 17th and 18th Centuries!

Young People

The battle for freedom of speech has been replaced by the battle for freedom of thought. Never, ever, check your minds at the door!

Wake up and pay attention to your lives! Look around and see who among you is both *peaceful* and *prosperous*. Adopt him or her as a mentor for your life. Your parents are a blessing, but their psychology of parenthood gets in their way. Have faith in your parents! Do their bidding and accept their guidance. Do not misuse their unconditional love. Be respectful to your parents, but adopt mentors outside your family.

Only you know how you feel. So, even as you economize time and money, keep in touch with yourselves. The trick to life is enjoying the moment, and not wasting the moment on unhealthy habits. Get out of the habit of depending on your parents for your good feelings, and find joy in yourselves.

Be thankful. Gratitude is a great attitude. Gratitude is a fleeting emotion among the unbelievers. Remember your debts to your ancestors and to humanity. Respect your elders. And, once you become financially self-sufficient, you should lovingly expand the worldviews of your parents.

Baby Boomers of America

Go back to your youth. Wake up to the conversation of your parents after the Second World War. They came home and talked about making love, not war. You heard them, and your psyches echoed their wishes in the 1960s.

Then you became busy with the lives of your children. Now they have gone and you are alone. Be with Me and at peace with yourselves. You created the peace movement of the 1960s, and you are the generation that can use the Internet to bring peace to humanity. Bestow this honor upon yourselves.

Professionals of the World

A foolish consistency is the hobgoblin of little minds. Great souls speak what they think today, and what they think tomorrow.

Few who have made it in politics did so because they were worthy. The politicians of today are the bronze class of Socrates. Many are allowing themselves to be used by others.

This is not a time for you to look "good" about money, time and intellectuality. This is a time for you to speak up. Do not make the mistake of dismissing yourselves, for that is the biggest sin you can commit against Me.

Businesspeople

You are far slower at adapting than you think. Update your worldviews frequently. Your very survival is now dependent upon your ability to adapt as quickly as possible.

Technology and trade are creating direct conversations across ancient cultures through a wide information highway that is getting wider by the month. Between cell phones and the Internet, the chatter is deafening. Slow down your chatter about how to make more money. Save your time for real chats with family and friends.

Devote some of the communication to non-business matters. When you allocate some of your chat to non-business matters, you are friendlier and business works better. Focus your non-business chat on understanding the beliefs, the history, and the culture of the person with whom you are speaking. Understand the environment in which he or she is living. Stop limiting your attention only to the business at hand.

The Wealthy and Powerful

Those of you who are very rich and powerful probably deserve it. But I must caution you that you are running into a potential safety problem. Privacy is the first casualty of the Information age. Security does not lie behind walls.

Practically all of humanity is now watching real-time audio-visual newscasts even though some are censored in some countries. This situation is not going to last. The Internet is going to make available to every person in your country the news that is published in any other country. Soon, even the ordinary citizen will be able to connect the dots. This will cause worldwide reality to become transparent. Your private dealings will start showing up. Even though things are done undercover and in secrecy, the overall results give away the cause.

Be careful and start being more considerate of others. This is in your best interest.

You are rich and powerful. Remember, however, everything that you own, owns you. That goes for money and that goes for political position. Pay attention to Benjamin Franklin and Mahatma Gandhi—neither of them occupied influential political offices. They did not want to be owned by the position they occupied. Albert Einstein politely declined the presidency of Israel, for he did not want to be owned.

The same logic applies to too much money. If you have accumulated a nest egg that will make you comfortable for the rest of your life, then there is not much point in making more money. It will only cause you grief. The Indian civilization is on to this. They have a saying, "Money is like the dirt on your hands." It is hard to have clean hands if you have too much money.

The Internet is making information available on any topic, to an unprecedented number of people. Obtaining useful information, and understanding trails of motivation, is making it difficult to do things you once could do privately.

Humanity is rapidly realizing that the economic power of business has just overtaken nation-states in their economic power. There is a rising swell. Protect your position and power by being cooperative and charitable.

The Curious

Stop watching TV or what pops up on your homepage! Widen your worldview by checking major worldwide newspapers on the Internet.

Stop listening to the gatekeepers of thought in your country. Know what is really going on in the world.

Peace is cooperation rather than competition; to become a part of a synergistic, living whole. It is learning to listen and live by conscience.

—Stephen R. Covey, American Author and
Business Consultant

20

To Governments

America

You were born as the most wonderful government known to humanity. But now you must improve. Having won the Cold War, do not let the corrupting forces that naturally come with being a superpower sway you. This is your greatest challenge. Live responsibly, or your human rights system of the late twentieth century may give way to a reign of terror akin to the French Revolution. Live up to the ideals of the Founding Fathers along with Emerson, Thoreau and Abraham Lincoln.

Use your own energy resources and stop meddling in other countries' affairs. Existence has no guarantees. You are selling your future and humanity's future in the name of "political correctness" and a counter-productive legal system.

Hold a Constitutional Convention. The earlier you do it, the better off you will be. Create a new Constitution from scratch. Do it now, and do it in an orderly way, or the people of America could rise up in revolution.

Do not confuse hard work, good luck, strength and prosperity with intelligence and wisdom. Your politicians are talking about building a bridge to the 21st century. Rather, focus on laying a foundation for the 21st century and beyond.

England

You gave the world the English language, an essential gift, for language is the second closest bond after blood. Now, turn your focus to how the English language can help the world communicate for greater understanding.

Israel

Demonstrate the leadership of your people by being magnanimous to your neighbors. It may be the beginning of something great for you and for the rest of the world.

Europe

Good job. Except for a few mishaps, you are an example of the opportunity for people of various languages and cultures to live together in peace.

China

Great economic progress, but what about human rights? Listen and take care of your children. They are your true resource for the future.

India

You have been independent for a while now. Market your intelligence and respect yourselves.

PART IV

EVOLUTION
through a sense of urgency
using intellect and
diplomacy.

Government is too big and too important to be left to the politicians.

—Chester Bowles, former Governor of the State of Connecticut and
U.S. Diplomat

21

California Leadership

In my opinion, the greatest statement of the 20th century came from Walt Kelly (and was later used by a WWII general), creator of the *Pogo* comic strip, who wrote, "We have met the enemy, and he is us." Recognizing that every entity is its own best friend—and yet its own worst enemy—is a profound insight. But having this insight alone doesn't help, for one cannot operate from outside one's head. So how does one help America continue its existence? Everyone, I am sure, would agree that evolution is better than revolution.

Growth occurs in spurts. But in modern times, people tend to fight nature. How does one go about bringing rapid but controlled change to a nation that is the most powerful on earth?

The way to do this is to pay attention to the realizations of ancient civilizations. Such civilizations have their own lessons of global superpower status, as well as their own colloquial sayings which make sense, "from outside the [mental] box" of the English language.

An insightful American colonel once told me, "If you find yourself in a hole, stop digging." That's another way of expressing how our own mental blind spots become our enemies. The second part of that saying is, "What is the cure for my condition? A friend." The notion here is that one cannot help oneself, for if one had that ability, one would have already pulled out of the hole one was in.

Now, every person who befriends you does not have the depth or the capability to help you out of the hole you find yourself in. Only a select few are capable. In my view, California is such a friend to America. I would even include Nevada with California as the entity that can and will help the United States cope responsibly and effectively with the difficult task of managing the world. California and Nevada are more adaptable than other states. Psychological clarity is abundant in California and Nevada. This gives them an edge. California's history-making governor's recall and gubernatorial election are recent examples of the state's ascendancy through the people's will.

"Managing" the world is a duty that America inherited by winning the Cold War. The situation was akin to having a baby. The parent is responsible for the baby; that is the natural order of things. But it seems that America has not paid attention to the words of The Duke of Wellington, the man who defeated Napoleon. He said, "Wars won are costlier than wars lost."

Having been in business for twenty years, I know a little bit about managing an entity in which your power is beyond challenge. Management requires "getting work done through other people." The inexperienced manager focuses on "through other people." The experienced manager focuses on "getting work done." During the last decade, America seems to have been acting as an inexperienced manager. That doesn't mean that America has to be a bully. It means that it has to take charge and make the right adjustments within itself, and then do the right things with others to make it happen.

Experienced "superpowers" must keep in mind the reality that everyone is too scared to tell you the bad news, so you have to be extra careful and extra responsible.

The oil magnates of Texas are ignoring California at their own peril. The high cost of oil-generated electricity in California is connected to the state's liberal voting past. California, on its own, claims to be the fifth largest economy in the world. California cannot be taken lightly.

Earlier in this book, I pointed out a historical fact of predictive importance. Just as America won the "cold war" when it was assigned telecommunications code 1 among the world's codes for telecommunication systems, California won its conflict with the power centers of the eastern United States when it was assigned transportation code 1 within the country's Magellan Global Positioning System. Such power is earned, not given.

I have been pointing out California's lead to my friends since 1999. Such mega forces have a life of their own. Therefore, the historical 2003 California gubernatorial recall and election did not surprise me. California is struggling with its own burden of leadership. The fact that a man born and raised in the second world is now in the Governor's mansion is almost as unusual, as a man born and raised in the third world is writing this book to help America get out of the mess it is in.

We are living in a rapidly changing world. Reagan was an actor, and he made an effective president. Underestimating the power of celebrity would be a mistake. Celebrities in America are people who are highly adaptable. To survive effectively, all species in nature adapt. Those who refuse to adapt are acting at their own peril.

The time for California to lead is now, lest the tree in which it is nesting desta-bilize, much like those forces unleashed by Rousseau's 1762 book, *The Social Contract*, when the ordinary man slaughtered the aristocrat next door. There was a *Declaration of the Rights of Man* made in France, at the same time America was busy re-drafting the *Articles of Confederation* into the *Constitution of the United States*.

A few hundred years later, there are still stark similarities between France of the late eighteenth century and the world of today. A new reign of terrorism has dawned, even as a focus has been brought to human rights. However, declaring war on terrorism is like declaring war on the planet. Better to "seek yourself inside yourself"; understand what adjustments can be made to our own policies in fairness to all nations, and let diplomacy and respect guide the way.

The mass of men lead lives of quiet desperation.

—Henry David Thoreau,
American author, poet and philosopher

22

Urgent!

In case you've missed the sense of urgency behind the message of this book, let me share some experiences I've had that should cure you of complacency.

In 1974, I bought a car in Frankfurt, Germany, and drove it to Pakistan. As I crossed Europe, Turkey and Iran, two things dawned upon me.

First, the time it took to travel across the whole of Europe was equal to the time it took to travel across Turkey and Iran. The second thing I remember is that there was something different about the people of Iran. They were the only people I had ever seen driving intentionally on the wrong side of the road.

Later, on assignment for an American company, I spent another seven months in Iran, working on their first nuclear power plant. Whenever I would say, "I'm from America," people would politely move on. But when I said, "I am from Pakistan," people would warm up, telling me, "You are my brother." After I left the country, a *revolution* happened. The regime, which had been supported by the United States for 25 years, was toppled. Khomeini took Iran back at least 200 years by running the state through the mosque. It sounded like they wanted anything but America.

I'm sensing similar conversations and attitudes in America now. As I speak to people in America about the American government, I get almost the same kind of response that I got in Iran many years ago. My sense is that a revolution may happen within a decade.

Why have a revolution when one can easily bring about evolutionary change through intellect and diplomacy? Only walls, like the wall of ineffective communication, create revolutions. Although I know the word is a derivative of "revolt," I like to think it comes from "Re-wall-utions."

Intellectual and evolutionary change can only be brought about through a sense of urgency. How do I know that? Let me tell you another story.

My business, now twenty years old, works for the U.S. Army Corps of Engineers (USACE). In the late 1990s, I sensed a positive change in the collective personality of the USACE. I was surprised because large groups do not change that quickly, especially those made up of engineers (like myself). So I started looking for the source of the change. That took me to the man who was then leading the organization, General Joe Ballard. I asked him if he had brought about the change intentionally. He said that he had, and showed me a book called, *Leading Change*, which says the very first step to creating change is creating a sense of urgency.

I tried to convince General Ballard to run for president in 2004. He is a great leader, and I believe America is ready for an African-American president. However, he politely declined. This is too bad, because a sense of urgency is exactly what America needs.

As noted earlier, even though man has landed on the moon many times, and any decent scientist can create a schedule for the moon's cycles in any part of the world, all Muslims will continue to look up to the skies for the beginning and ending of the month of Ramadan. Similarly, although the Vatican has had to reverse its positions on Galileo, the British Monarchy and Darwin, and was essentially ignored by the Founding Fathers of America, it continues to be revered by Christians. And when a Jewish psychiatrist I know speaks of the Ten Commandments, it is with a difference in his attitude that is hard to define.

This is not the time, however, to invoke religion; nor is it a time to invoke too much patriotism.

As any couple that has been to relationship counseling knows, the best way to handle an argument is to take a break when emotions are running high. Once emotions have subsided, a reasonable discussion can continue. The emotions of the East and West are running high right now, and it is important **and** urgent that we take a break to calm down, before something more terrible happens.

It isn't enough to talk about peace. One must believe in it. And it isn't enough to believe in it. One must work at it.

    —Eleanor Roosevelt, Social Activist, former U.S. Representative to the United Nations, and first lady to Franklin D. Roosevelt

23

Toward Solutions—Redux

My children know me better than anyone else. On September 21, 2003, my 11-year-old son decided to improve my productivity by giving me a deadline. The deadline was that I must become famous within a year. As I stepped up to the challenge, the real solution dawned on me on the morning of September 23, 2003.

I started implementing my solution to the problem of world peace the next day. I am now "doing business as" My Use International (My Use).

My Use, first intended to be an international political party, has begun operating as a company in the business of achieving world peace through the promotion of mutual understanding among the world's diverse cultures. We plan to do this with thought-provoking entertainment and education in the forms of comedy, drama, adventure, biographies, artistic images, poetry and music. And we will do it by utilizing the written and spoken word as well as film, CD, video and DVD. One of our services on the World Wide Web will be identity verification and birth/death certifications, which are problems of the first order.

My Use contacted the U.S. Department of Defense (DoD) in December 2003 about creating/adopting a Department of Peace. It was at the time of a conference in Washington, DC for small business participation in DoD contracting in the U.S. and for the reconstruction effort in Iraq. Through General Ballard and General Flowers, My Use was asked to prepare a White Paper which was sent to them in abstract form. The full text of this appears in Part 5 of this book.

My Use is for the use of humanity, and it can operate with a slow, steady and legitimate growth. Naturally, I intend to get out of the way of "ownership of the business" as soon as possible, for my intention is to create a vehicle that can be used effectively by others. I envision Internet chat sessions, question and answer postings, printed materials that can be downloaded freely about peace topics and organizations, automated language translation in order to allow those of all cultures to communicate with each other, and current information postings about business and nation-state happenings that pertain to national and international policies that may affect our collective wellbeing. This Internet organization can generate huge political power, if coordinated steadily and properly; this will give enough strength to the people of the world to influence their politicians towards governing for the benefit of the masses, rather than the business or political elites.

I may be an experienced businessman, but I am an amateur savior. I need all the help I can get. Please visit us at www.myuse.org and join us by sending an e-mail telling us how you can help—because the rest is up to you.

We must dream of an aristocracy of achievement in a democracy of opportunity.

—Thomas Jefferson, Author of the Declaration of Independence
and 3rd President of the United States

24

Your Attention Needed

Having been raised in the cradle of the British civilization's remnants, the words, "Your attention, please," hold a special meaning within my psyche.

Attention is the most difficult thing to get in America. Even celebrities end up doing strange things to keep their names in the limelight (e.g. running for political office without real intent; baring breasts on family-time national TV). I could not even get the attention of my neighbors or members of the local city council on the very important topics I have discussed in this book.

But I keep thinking of Ronald Reagan who quoted Rabbi Hillel, who asked: "If not us, then who; and if not now, then when?"

There is always some risk, whether emotionally, physically or spiritually, in writing about our deepest feelings and most passionate concerns, exposing our souls to the world at large. But, if it makes one more person think about the road to peace, it is a risk worth taking.

As Don McLean sang wistfully in his song, *Vincent (Starry Starry Night)*:

> "Now I think I know
> What you tried to say to me,
> And how you suffered for your sanity,
> And how you tried to set them free.
> They would not listen.
> They're not listening still.
> Perhaps they never will…"

PART V

EMANCIPATION
from politics as usual.

A good understanding of language and civilization beats ten thousand years of bad psychology.

—I. Khan

25

Language is Key

Chapter 1 of this book (*Worldviews*) discusses the concept behind the theory of relativity and how Einstein applied it to look outside the commonly accepted notion of reality with respect to the speed of light. You'll recall my statement that I'm applying the same concept and looking outside physics, philosophy, politics and psychology.

What does this mean? The answer lies in understanding the role of language in human affairs. Of all the tools and technology created by mankind, language is the most profound and useful. Everyone knows reading, writing, and arithmetic are the fundamental skills of life. Each of these requires the use of language. While mathematics and accounting are different kinds of languages, they were constructed because spoken language created the faculty. It is due to language that the average man of today is living more comfortably than the kings of only two centuries ago who did not have access to telephones, electricity, air conditioning, airplanes, etc.

We are so comfortable with the usefulness of spoken language that it's difficult to accept the reality that most conflicts are created by language. I have had my share of problems with this interesting phenomenon. Years ago, I lost all hope and occasionally courted suicidal thoughts. The only reason a person would commit suicide is if he were in total despair and has convinced himself that living is more painful than ending it all. Now let me ask you: How could I have convinced myself that there is no hope in the future? The only way I could have done this was by thoughtful reflection in a *conversation* with myself. That devastating self-conversation required a language for expression. All the evidence clearly pointed to a situation from which there was no escape.

Had I never learned to speak a language, there is no way I could have found myself in that position. The culprit was language. Language had created unchecked self-talk in my head, which had given me so many unnecessary sleepless nights. If, as a person, I can allow language to trick me into ending my life as an individual, imagine what language can do to nations.

◆   ◆   ◆

The modern science of neuro-linguistic programming (NLP) states that an average person's neural pathways are like a computer program. In other words, we script ourselves at an early age to process information in a certain way. We use that way of processing for the rest of our lives without realizing what we're doing. We learn to talk to ourselves in a certain way. Some of us are respectful to ourselves, and others are not. Those who talk to themselves respectfully live a happy life. Those who do not are the ones we call, "hard on themselves."

The book *NLP: The New Technology of Achievement* asserts that we can create new neural pathways by the application of certain thought exercises so that the programs (ways of thought) of our brains are versatile. In other words, if I've been operating on Microsoft Word all my life, I can, using techniques described in *NLP,* add the capability of Microsoft Excel, Microsoft Outlook, and other software. Thus, an expert in NLP can choose the proper application program (response) for the right situation.

Two personal experiences of mine confirmed the claims of the proponents of NLP. Both times I had a near-death experience, and the last words that came to my mind were *Allah-o-Akbar.* They mean "God is Great," which is a statement of acceptance. My conclusion is that these words had been programmed into my mind to provide a stable foundation for my psyche. I now suspect that the role of language in human affairs is even greater than I had estimated.

◆   ◆   ◆

It's difficult to think outside of language. It can be done, but most of us are spending most of our thinking time using languages. This is the reason people tell us to think positive so that we can feel good. Thinking positive is nothing more than having a positive conversation with yourself. It's easier to talk about this skill than to actually internalize it. Anyway, this book is not about trying to help you learn this skill. It is about making you realize that if the conversations of man could be brought to a standstill, most conflict and violence would vanish.

The only real problems of life are food, water and safety. How many of you are feeling hungry, thirsty or unsafe as you read this book? Meanwhile, we have all kinds of other belief systems, upon which we build our psychologies and thought patterns that cause us unending grief. Realizing this, I asked myself what would happen if I emptied my mind of all previous beliefs, as did Rene Descartes. Not only that, I also chose to empty my mind of words. Much to my surprise, I developed an ability to stop thinking at will. All I do is visualize myself as an object, such as a stone; and lo and behold, I enter into the now. What I discovered with this thought exercise was that thoughts are just words we speak to ourselves. Without the presence of words, thoughts abated. Without words and thoughts in my psyche, I felt calm and peaceful, and more accepting of myself, as well as everyone else.

I've never meditated for long periods of time, but I've heard from people who regularly do, that, if you meditate for several days, "The chatter in your head dies down." I expect the resultant feelings must be similar.

◆　　　◆　　　◆

The most rigorous of all sciences is physics. Physicists do not believe anything until it is proven over and over again by a variety of researchers. Physicists are well aware that the early Greek philosophers became so credible that their mistakes set physics back centuries. Physics successfully overturned their proclamations and edicts, but it took centuries to accomplish this. Therefore, physicists often summarize the significance of their efforts by saying, "One good *observation* of physics beats a century of bad philosophy." Thus, one realizes how languages create shared beliefs, which are so hard to overturn that it takes centuries of experimentation. Physics uses the precise language of mathematics, while philosophy uses spoken language. As I said earlier, I was beginning to suspect the shortcomings of spoken language.

I started extending in my own mind the thought process expressed by physicists. Soon, I came up with a personal statement that went something like, "One good *concept or idea* beats a millennium of bad politics." For example, the idea of separating church and state had more power than the thousand years of political development that preceded it.

Extrapolating the same line of thinking, I came up with another statement: "A good understanding of *language and civilization* beats ten thousand years of bad psychology."

Without language, I was one with the universe and nature, and the need to judge others or myself disappeared. At that point, I sensed I was looking outside language. By looking outside language, I was actually looking outside physics, politics, and psychology, because they are only constructs of language. I will grant that physics is a little different because it relies on mathematics; but then, mathematics is also constructed by language.

The conflicts in the world in which we live continue to indicate that politics as usual is not an option, and that our understanding of language and how we use it can play a great part toward more peaceful solutions.

If you succumb to the temptation of using violence in the struggle, unborn generations will be the recipients of a long and desolate night of bitterness, and your chief legacy to the future will be an endless reign of meaningless chaos.

—Martin Luther King, Jr., American Civil Rights Activist

26

Nuclear Terrorism

Following the fall of the Soviet Union, many nuclear devices were accounted. Some of them were in portable suitcases. No one knows for sure whether terrorist organizations have possession and control of any such weapons.

It would be prudent to keep in mind that there is a parallel between the 1990 invasion of Kuwait by Saddam Hussein and the 2001 events by Osama bin Laden. Both occurred shortly after an oilman was elected president.

September 11 has changed the world. The pre-emptive American attack on Iraq has caused emotional stress worldwide. Therefore, it is not prudent to rule out the possibility of a nuclear weapon detonation in a large American city should an oilman be elected again.

George Bush is a willful and strong leader. We are living in times that require unusual acts of leadership. Mikhail Gorbachev stood down to end the Cold War. Al Gore conceded to avoid confusion. Both of these were acts of leadership in their own way. George Bush could go down in history as a great American president if he would choose to go for the moral high ground and allow another Republican to run, in spite of obvious party pressures.

The election of 2004 and the events of 2005 may define history in a larger way than did September 11, 2001.

The current emphasis on fighting terrorism is like taking our eyes off the road to swat a fly on the car window while a truck is headed straight for the car.

—I. Khan

27

The Department of Defense

As one who follows the US Department of Defense, I was interested to see a memorandum to General Dick Myers (and others) from the current chief, Donald Rumsfeld, which was leaked to the press in October 2003. It was immediately reproduced in all the major newspapers, as it appears below.

Los Angeles Times   October 23, 2003

RUMSFELD'S MEMO

'Are We Winning or Losing the…War on Terror?'
Below is the full text of Defense Secretary Donald H. Rumsfeld's Oct. 16 memo on the war on terrorism:

TO:	**Gen. Dick Myers, Paul Wolfowitz, Gen. Pete Pace, Doug Feith**
FROM:	**Donald Rumsfeld**
SUBJECT:	**Global War on Terrorism**

The questions I posed to combatant commanders this week were: Are we winning or losing the Global War on Terror? Is DoD changing fast enough to deal with the new 21st century security environment? Can a big institution change fast enough? Is the USG changing fast enough?

DoD has been organized, trained and equipped to fight big armies, navies and air forces. It is not possible to change DoD fast enough to successfully fight the global war on terror; an alternative might be to try to fashion a new institution, either within DoD or elsewhere—one that seamlessly focuses the capabilities of several departments and agencies on this key problem.

With respect to global terrorism, the record since September 11th seems to be:

- We are having mixed results with Al Qaida, although we have put considerable pressure on them—nonetheless, a great many remain at large.
- USG has made reasonable progress in capturing or killing the top 55 Iraqis.
- USG has made somewhat slower progress tracking down the Taliban—(fugitive leader Mullah Mohammad Omar, Afghan warlord Gulbuddin, Hekmatyar, etc.)
- With respect to the Ansar Al-Islam, we are just getting started.

Have we fashioned the right mix of rewards, amnesty, protection and confidence in the US?

Does DoD need to think through new ways to organize, train, equip and focus to deal with the global war on terror?

Are the changes we have and are making too modest and incremental? My impression is that we have not yet made truly bold moves, although we have made many sensible, logical moves in the right direction, but are they enough?

Today, we lack metrics to know if we are winning or losing the global war on terror. Are we capturing, killing or deterring and dissuading more terrorists every day than the *madrassas* (Islamic schools) and the radical clerics are recruiting, training and deploying against us?

Does the US need to fashion a broad, integrated plan to stop the next generation of terrorists? The US is putting relatively little effort into a long-range plan, but we are putting a great deal of effort into trying to stop terrorists. The cost-benefit ratio is against us! Our cost is billions against the terrorists' costs of millions.

- Do we need a new organization?
- How do we stop those who are financing the radical *madrassa* schools?
- Is our current situation such that "the harder we work, the behinder we get"?

It is pretty clear that the coalition can win in Afghanistan and Iraq in one way or another, but it will be a long, hard slog.

Does CIA need a new finding?

Should we create a private foundation to entice radical *madrassas* to a more moderate course?

What else should we be considering?
Please be prepared to discuss this at our meeting on Saturday or Monday.

Thanks.

Source: Department of Defense

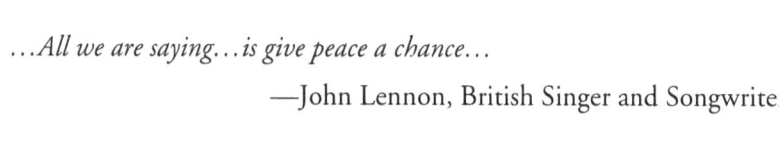

…All we are saying…is give peace a chance…

—John Lennon, British Singer and Songwriter

28

A Suggestion

My Use International issued the following letter to the United States Department of Defense on October 24, 2003.

My Use International

22632 Golden Springs Drive, #240
Diamond Bar, CA 91765

Phone: 909/396-7662
Fax: 909/396-1455

October 24, 2003

Honorable Donald H. Rumsfeld
Secretary of Defense
1000 Defense Pentagon
Washington, DC 20301-1000

Dear Mr. Rumsfeld:

The leak of the Rumsfeld memorandum to America continues to erode the psychological superpower status of America, leading toward an unstable world in which World War III becomes a stronger possibility. The Muslim resistance to Western control of its oil will rise as the news of this memorandum ripples through the psychology of one quarter of the human race. Silently, they are cheering Osama as well as Saddam, even though they don't like Saddam.

This is a problem that America seems to be confused about. What America does not know is that the war is not between America and Islam; it is between English and Arabic. The Jewish people are living in the year 5764. One of their two major leaders was Moses. Moses was a fan of the number 10. Not only did he come back with the Ten Commandments, he also organized his armies by a span of control of ten. This means he had ten people reporting to him, and each one of the ten people had ten people reporting to them, and so on.

What America and DoD don't know is that thousands of years ago, some of the Zion people went east, and later converted to Islam. They are called, "Pukhtoons." There are about 35 million in the world; 20 million in Pakistan, and 15 million in Afghanistan. The collective subconscious of these people is that they brought down Alexander the Great, the Mogul Dynasty of India, the British Empire, the government of Pakistan, and the Soviet Union. Once they hear about Rumsfeld's memorandum, they are likely to be very happy.

I come from this tribe and I would like to help America. Nobody has talked about this tribe in the news. The only superpower that ever dealt reasonably well with this group was the Mogul Dynasty of India. They elected to make friends with the Pukhtoons and make them responsible for security within their transportation systems.

If America wishes to move forward positively, it would be a good idea to approach the Pukhtoons in a friendly way to see if they would like to take on the responsibility of the world's transportation system.

Since I have lived in America and have worked with the Department of Defense for twenty years, I think I can convince the Pukhtoons to do that. In my opinion, this would be a win-all situation and perhaps we can bring an end to war of mankind.

Sincerely,
I. Khan

◆   ◆   ◆

To our pleasant surprise the US Army Corps of Engineers (a part of DoD) requested a White Paper from My Use. The following White Paper was submitted.

My Use International

23632 Golden Springs Drive, #240
Diamond Bar, CA 91765

Phone: 909/860-4332
Fax: 909/961-2311
Info@MyUse.org

November 21, 2003

White Paper

For review and comment by General Ballard:

Introduction

We at My Use International are deeply honored at the request from the U.S. Army Corps of Engineers leadership to submit a white paper on the topic of managing the world situation. The widely published memorandum by Donald Rumsfeld indicates that the Department of Defense is trying hard, but is structurally incapable of changing fast enough to deal with guerilla warfare. Nobody is at fault. We must accept the situation as it is.

It is human nature to go into psychological denial at a time like this. American leadership cannot afford the time lost in adjusting to reality. The book *Who Moved My Cheese*, which is on the subject of change management, is right on the money.

Our letter to Donald Rumsfeld's office, which was copied to major newspapers, is also attached. We are confident that we can convert this lose-all situation into a win-all situation.

The relationship between General Ballard and I. Khan has created this opportunity to present ideas to responsible people at the Department of Defense. We are impressed with the openness of the Department of Defense.

This document is just an outline of ideas. Please keep in mind that it is not a full-blown plan. Please also keep in mind that even after a full-blown plan is developed, 15% comes from the planning and 85% comes from the implementation. *Time Magazine* reports that we are reaching out to the Taliban (November 10 issue). That is what we had suggested in our open letter dated October 24, 2003, but if that is the implementation, it is not the best way.

Parameters

Any attempt to bring the currently out-of-control spiral of violence, terrorism, and costly reprisals to an end must have the following elements:

1. America's superpower must be maintained. America is the beacon of hope for the world at this time. Instability in America will only result in instability worldwide.

2. Jewish people will need the strongest assurances about their future, their acceptance, their security, and their freedom because their collective understanding of history is indeed worrisome.

3. The Muslims of the world, in general, and those in Palestine, Afghanistan, Iraq, and Saudi Arabia in particular, must be acknowledged and calmed down. Acknowledgement is necessary because the root cause of all violence is a real or perceived lack of acceptance. This does not mean yielding to terrorist actions; what it does mean is thinking outside the box.

4. America's current worldwide image as a belligerent, out-of-control superpower, which is a threat not only to the third world but also to the European Union, must be addressed and brought back to reality. Americans are warm, friendly and generous and we believe in "live and let live." The American people do not necessarily condone the recent actions of the government, especially in Iraq.

To achieve the above four objectives, anyone born and raised in America will not have enough perspective to be able to think of inexpensive, effective solutions, much less implement them. Fortunately, in this rapidly evolving world, I. Khan happened to have spent the first 21 years in Pakistan and the last 35 years in North America. The direct 20-year long business relationship with the DoD and links with the high-tech Silicon Valley firms through the organization called TiE are also helpful. All this provides a perspective and a solution that would be almost impossible for someone born in America to have and reach.

Situation

Before going into the solutions to the problem, one must look into the causes. The Muslim population of the world is the fastest growing of the major religions; every fourth person on this planet is a Muslim. The overall condition of the Muslims, however, is indeed sad. This is so in spite of the fact that they have tremendous oil reserves (modern gold) in the Persian Gulf and in Central Asia. The weakness of the Muslim world did not just happen by chance. The nations of Islam would be well advised to take responsibility. They have made a historical mistake; continuing to mix church and state. This is understandable because the *Qur'an* mixes church and state. Nevertheless, life moves forward and not backward. When the West separated church and state, the Age of Reason created phenomenal progress and power, which translated into a better lifestyle. The Muslims only have themselves to look at for their current situation.

One can take the attitude that "somebody else did it to me" or one can say, "I was sleeping and I should not have been sleeping." The second way of thinking is much better because you can choose to wake up. The first way of thinking is not useful because it builds resentment to the point that young people end up killing themselves, and does not produce any tangible benefit.

There is only one Jewish person for every 400 Christians, Muslims, Hindus, and Buddhists, combined, in this world. In spite of this 1/400 ratio, the Jewish people have succeeded so well that their influence equals that of the other four religions. Everyone must understand that nobody gave these people handouts on a silver platter. They worked hard and they're reaping the rewards for their hard work. There are two suggestions that I have for this highly competent minority that might help. First, they should advertise the fact that they are living in the 6th millennium. Once people know that fact, they will not judge them so harshly. Everyone knows that the Jewish people think of themselves as the chosen ones. Such an attitude is natural. Any one of us living in the 6th millennium would feel special compared to the rest of the human race that is only in the 3rd millennium.

The second bit of advice I have for the Jewish people is to relax and understand that history will not repeat itself and that they will not be persecuted one more time. But it is up to them to make this happen. Everybody must take responsibility. I have learned in my life that every time I start thinking of myself as a victim, I become unhappy, and I end up wallowing in miserable self-pity. It does not help my feelings nor does it help my future. Therefore, I have learned to realize that we are all born into this world defenseless, and that as we grow, we do the best we can for ourselves. Everybody acts in self-interest. To avoid a repeat of persecution in a few decades the Jews must get out of the victim mentality. They will find peace immediately within their souls, and their children will be warmly accepted instead of persecuted.

The sole superpower status is traditionally difficult to maintain. Nobody sympathizes with a leader. Historically, the only superpower that dealt successfully with terrorism (guerilla warfare) was the Mogul dynasty, which made friends with the Pukhtoons and paid them handsomely to maintain security of the transportation systems throughout their empire. The Pukhtoons felt honored and were, of course, paid. The plan worked like a charm. The terrorism stopped. Such plans must be implemented with care and dexterity. The Mogul dynasty attempted the same with another group that waged guerrilla warfare but never approached them in a respectful way. That is supposed to be one of the causes of the downfall of the Mogul empire.

Now I'm going to provide an outline of a plan. Please do not jump to conclusions about the plan until you have read the follow-up explanation and logic behind each of the steps.

THE OUTLINE OF A PLAN

The implementation of this plan will require the creation of a Department of Peace within or outside of the Department of Defense. In the new state of the planet, the public affairs of man that used to be documented by the highly respected magazine *Foreign Affairs,* have now taken on the modality of internal affairs.

The very use of the words, "Department of Peace" will send a message not only to the Muslims but also to the rest of the world that America is not a warmongering nation. Perhaps it would be a good idea to conduct trade in the newly constructed WTC buildings but use the name, "World Peace Center" instead of, "World Trade Center." This is not the time for bravado and face-saving. This very small gesture will pay off big. The people who continue to attack the World Trade Center will get the message that we are beginning to work on peaceful trade.

Now let me address each element of the plan one-by-one.

1. The Department of Peace should be staffed with enlightened Muslim-Americans, to form at least 20-30% of its total staff.

2. Negotiations should be started immediately with not only the Pukhtoons but also Muslim tribes, which may be capable and interested in taking on the task of transportation security worldwide. At least 3-4 different groups should be contacted in the spirit of competition. Some training may be required but this may be a small investment. The salaries of these people are going to be so low compared to the salaries of

American DoD employees that the result will be a tiny fraction of the cost.

3.   I am volunteering my services to lead this effort.

4.   The Israeli and Jewish population of the world should be invited to participate in the final planning of this activity. However, they should not be a part of the implementation.

5.   Funding will have to be released at a substantial level at the outset so that such a department can be brought into existence in short order. Should such funding be available, I am quite confident that I can organize and run such a department. Some of the Iraq reconstruction money, if approved for this purpose, would be a great message. Congress can provide an exception.

THE WISDOM BEHIND THE PLAN

Now we will examine each of the above points and the thought process behind them.

1.   You may not believe it, but millions of Muslim-Americans are living in terror in the United States at this time. I could not get them to support the peace march on the last Martin Luther King birthday. Therefore, there are many educated people who would jump at the opportunity to make a positive difference. I am from this community, and not only can I access it, but I can screen it.

   If you have any concerns that these people will end up being terrorist cells within the Department of Peace, I must admonish you that nobody wants war. Such thinking is paranoid. Paranoid thinking will lead us into hell. Since there are no guarantees in life, these people can actually be monitored because there are only a few of them. The wisdom behind this approach is that the world's Islamic community will feel acknowledged, honored, and made a part of the solution instead of part of the problem. This kind of attitude has a calming effect on people.

2.   There is rampant unemployment in the Muslim world. People, if approached with tact, honor and dignity, will jump at the opportunity to compete for this. I know the value system of these people. They're far more committed when they take on responsibility. They will do a good

job once they are trained. The wisdom behind this action is that the Muslim population of the rest of the world will realize that America is not about religion—it is about state. During these negotiations I would make it a big point to tell them how America came to the rescue of Muslims in Bosnia and Kosovo. After all, everyone wants to become part of the economic system. Right now they are feeling left out. Who cares about who controls oil as long as people are economically well off? Such exclusivity is the longing of the Islamic mentality.

3. The only reason I am putting myself into this very difficult position for which no sane person would want to volunteer, is that first, there is too much at stake; and second, I am unique. I have been in a continuous business relationship with the DoD for many decades. Most conflict arises because of the inability of both sides to comprehend the actions of the other. I can understand and explain things to both sides. Yet, I cannot guarantee success.

4. It is absolutely necessary to have active participation from the Jewish community, because that way they will accept the plan and can bring a lot of intelligence and wisdom to the finalization of the plan. Their involvement will give them ownership to support this activity. The reason I do not suggest their participation in the implementation stage is that the hearts on both sides have become a little too hard. It is not a good idea to bring two highly charged bodies too close to each other.

5. The effort being suggested is not a small one. However, when compared with the results and the standards of the DoD's expenditures, it is miniscule. Without up-front funding nothing is going to happen. At this point, the DoD will have to think outside the box once more. These are unusual times requiring unusual responses.

The DoD is a process-driven organization. I understand this. There are checks and balances, the Code of Federal Regulations, and the Federal Acquisition Regulations to contend with, not to speak of the overlay of regulations created by the DoD. These will not permit the Department of Peace to succeed. Some regulation is all right but it would have to be negotiated with the budget appropriation committee so that the regulation does not choke the purpose. Not only is regulation expensive, it also causes time delay. The emotions flaring across the world must be calmed down immediately—there is no time to waste.

CONCLUDING COMMENTS

I am no diplomat; nor, I am an expert in foreign affairs. The only credibility I have is the validity of my success. I can learn on the job. Even as this white paper is discussed, a parallel book, *The Health of Nations,* is due for release soon. I can share with you selected chapters to assure you that I am operating out of a deeply reflective state of mind.

I was in Iran before the revolution. I remember the way people talked and acted. As of Halloween 2003, I am beginning to see the same type of actions and conversations in America. I am a proponent of evolution, not revolution. Therefore, I suggest prompt action to control the vehicle called the United States before it crashes. If that happens, nobody will come out ahead.

◆   ◆   ◆

We are currently awaiting a response from the DoD. It is not clear what their position will be.

This nation is the last great hope of mankind.

—Abraham Lincoln, 16th President of the United States

29

A Ray of Hope

More than a year later, My Use International has not received a response from the DoD, and George W. Bush has been elected for a second term. However, we see a major change in the foreign policy of the USA, and the resulting dynamics in world peace. Condoleezza Rice, now Secretary of State instead of National Security Advisor, is on a world tour of diplomacy in an effort to pull the USA out of its isolation from the rest of the world. The USA is not trying to do it alone, but is lobbying for support.

Iran is not being threatened with military action; instead, financial support is being offered in lieu of giving up nuclear pursuit. Israelis and Palestinians have entered into peace negotiations, and hostilities have dropped significantly. India and Pakistan are entering an unprecedented relationship of friendship. Syria is withdrawing its troops from Lebanon. We believe all of this could not have happened without a major shift in USA's foreign policy. We welcome this change in the policies of the Bush administration, and urge its continuation, even in the face of some possible setbacks. A more inclusive and comprehensive look at the world is bound to foster tolerance, understanding, and friendship.

We are at the crossroads now. There are two choices: one, a solution through force of arms; the other, through the most powerful force preached by Buddha, Abraham, Christ, and Muhammad—love of humanity. If we want to avoid Armageddon, we must not think nations and nationality; we must think love and humanity. Our world has become a 'Wasteland," where hypocrisy in the garbs of fundamentalism, neo-conservatism, and authoritarianism is trying to assert itself in various countries of the world, ours not excepted. Love and tolerance, is the only way to defeat the powers of these evils. Love, which is at the core of all religions has been hijacked, suppressed, and recycled so that the devious agendas of the few prevail over the wishes of the many. Let us take the fight to these people; let us say emphatically, we will not tolerate fanaticism; we will not tolerate injustice; we will not tolerate the annihilation of humanity. Let us say to "the tired, the oppressed, and the weary of the world," do not give up hope. We are here. We are My Use International. We will have PEACE!

Bibliography

Andreas, Steve and Charles Faulkner, ed. <u>NLP: The New Technology of Achievement</u>. New York: Morrow, 1994.

Ayub Khan, Mohammad. <u>Friends not Masters, a political autobiography</u>. N. Y., Oxford Univ. Press, 1967.

Canfield, Jack and Mark Victor Hansen [compilers]. <u>Chicken Soup for the Soul: 101 Stories to Open the Heart & Rekindle the Spirit</u>. Deerfield Beach, FL: Health Communications, 1993.

Chricton, Michael. <u>Timeline</u>. New York: Alfred A.Knopf, 1999.

Clancy, Tom. <u>Debt of Honor</u>. New York: G.P. Putnam's Sons, 1994.

—. <u>Executive Orders</u>. New York: Putnam's Sons, 1996.

Covey, Stephen R. <u>The 7 Habits of Highly Effective People: Restoring the Character Ethic</u>. New York: Simon & Schuster, 1989.

Downs, Elizabeth C. and Robert Bingham Downs. <u>American Humor</u>. Chapel Hill, N.C.: The University of North Carolina Press, 1938.

Eberstadt, Mary. <u>Home-Alone America: The Hidden Toll of Day Care, Wonder Drugs, and Other Parent Substitutes</u>. New York: Sentinel, 2004.

Engdahl, F. William. <u>A Century of War: Anglo-American Oil Politics and the New World Order</u>. Germany, Paul & Company Publishers Consortium, Inc., 1993.

Ferguson, Niall. <u>The Cash Nexus: Money and Power in the Modern World</u>. New York: Basic Books, 2001.

—. <u>Empire: The Rise and Demise of the British World Order and the Lessons for Global Power</u>. New York: Basic Books, 2003.

Goldberg, Bernard. <u>Bias: A CBS Insider Exposes How the Media Distorts the News</u>. Washington, DC: Regenry Pub., 2002.

Gray, John. <u>Men Are From Mars, Women Are From Venus: A Practical Guide for Improving Communications and Getting What You Want in Your Relationships</u>. New York: Harper Collins, 1992.

Jacobs, Joseph J. <u>The Compassionate Conservative: Seeking Responsibility and Human Dignity</u>. Lafayette, La: Huntington House Publishers, 1996.

Johnson, Spencer. <u>Who Moved My Cheese? : And Amazing Way to Deal with Change in Your Work and in Your Life</u>. New York: G.P. Putnam's Sons, 1998.

Jones, Alan B. <u>How the World Really Works</u>. Paradise, CA: ABJ Press, 1996.

Kotter, John P. <u>Leading Change</u>. Boston: Harvard Business School Press, 1996.

McGraw, Phillip C. <u>Life Strategies: Doing What Works, Doing What Matters</u>. New York: Hyperion Books, 1999.

Peck, M. Scott, <u>The Road Less Traveled: A New Psychology of Love, Traditional Values and Spiritual Growth</u>. New York: Simon & Schuster, 1978.

Peck, M. Scott, <u>The Different Drum: Community Making and Peace</u>. New York: Simon and Schuster, 1987.

Peck, M. Scott, <u>People of the Lie: The Hope for Healing Human Evil</u>. New York: Simon and Schuster, 1998.

Ries, Al and Jack Trout. <u>Positioning: The Battle for Your Mind</u>. New York, McGraw-Hill, 2001.

Rousseau, Jean-Jacques. <u>The Social Contract</u>. Harmondsworth: Penguin, 1968.

Schwartz, Tony. <u>Media, the Second God</u>. New York: Random House, 1981.

Smith, Adam. <u>An Inquiry into the Nature and Causes of the Wealth of Nations</u>. Buffalo, N.Y.: Prometheus Books, 1991.

Sunzi. <u>The Art of War</u>. London: Oxford University Press, 1963.

978-0-595-31997-8
0-595-31997-1

www.ingramcontent.com/pod-product-compliance
Lightning Source LLC
Chambersburg PA
CBHW061258280526
45784CB00002B/808